North American
Hunting Adventures

North American Hunting Adventures

Hunter's Information Series ®
North American Hunting Club
Minneapolis, Minnesota

North American Hunting Adventures

Library of Congress Catalog Card Number 87-0613212
ISBN 0-914697-09-9

Printed in U.S.A.
10   11   12   13   14   15   16   17   18   19

Contents

Acknowledgments

Of all the great books in the North American Hunting Club Hunter's Information Series™, this edition is most truly a members' book. It is written by NAHC members especially for fellow members to enjoy. Congratulations to all the members whose exciting North American hunting adventures make this book so memorable.

Special thanks to Associate Editor Steve Pennaz for the hours he spent helping the members get their stories down on paper in readable form. NAHC Executive Vice President Mark LaBarbera, Managing Editor Bill Miller, Member Products Manager Mike Vail and Project Coordinator Linda Kalinowski all made vital contributions in making *North American Hunting Adventures* a tremendous success.

Steven F. Burke
President
North American Hunting Club

Photo & Art Credits

The illustrations for *North American Hunting Adventures* are exclusive original pen and ink sketches done by Mark Mansanarez of Jackson, Wyoming. Most of the photos have been provided by the NAHC members who wrote the stories with which the photos appear. Live animal photos are the work of Judd Cooney and Leonard Lee Rue Enterprises.

Foreword

Though every hunt is exciting in and of itself, there are those trips afield that produce the stories we'll tell around the campfire for years to come. They are the tales of charging bears. Of monster whitetail bucks. Of hard earned bull caribou. Of record trophies that fall to first time hunters.

These are the stories which make up *North American Hunting Adventures*.

They are the true stories of NAHC members from across the country. They are the tales of adventure that will take your breath away. They are the kind of stories that will make you sit back and feel proud that we still have this kind of sport available in North America.

NAHC Associate Editor Steve Pennaz pulled together these adventures from records kept during the first 10 years of the North American Hunting Club. Nearly all the stories were candidates for the President's Trophy Award. Those with the special stamp at the beginning of the story were President's Trophy winners.

In bringing together *North American Hunting Adventures*, we relied heavily on Steve's rapport with NAHC members and on his judgment of "exciting." Steve corresponded a great deal with the members whose stories appear in this book to bring out just the right angle in each true story.

Steve drew on his own experiences in big game camps of the

NAHC Associate Editor Steve Pennaz, who compiled and edited the stories in **North American Hunting Adventures,** *took this black bear with his bow on a spring hunt in Ontario.*

West, Midwest and Canada; recalling the best tales of hunting adventure he has heard and experienced. He looked for the common thread of excitement in those stories and has woven it into each story in this edition.

Every North American Hunting Club member reading these tales knows the bite of the morning air boosts the tempo of his pulse every time he sets out into the woods. If it didn't, he wouldn't be hunting. Every day in camp with his close friends is an adventure. If it wasn't we wouldn't be hunting. At the close of every gameless season, he is already anticipating "next year." If he wasn't, he wouldn't be hunting.

'nough said.

But this book is dedicated to those exciting and special hunts that we can all look back on and remember as bona fide successes.

Introduction

I looked across the campfire into the tired eyes of my hunting companions. Cecil was poking at the fire trying to push a half-charred pine log into the rest of the flames. Some extra heat would feel good. September days in the high country of northern Idaho can warm into the 60s and 70s, but September nights like to drop into the 20s or 30s—sometimes even lower.

Tony sat on the log next to me, quietly finishing the contents of a steaming cup of black coffee. His Stetson was pushed back, hiding none of the weariness that showed on his face. Beside him on the log was an empty dinner plate. Empty, that is, if you looked beyond the pile of chicken bones resting atop the faded rose print and didn't notice the ripped potato skin that was hidden behind the carnage.

Elbo was sleeping. At least, I thought he was when I first looked over at him. But every once in a while, he would open his eyes, shake his head slightly and stare at something resting against a stump behind Cecil. Then he would close his eyes again and the rhythmic breathing would begin again. Occasionally a small smile would form and he would look strangely satisfied.

Cecil broke the silence.

"Elbo. How far was your shot this morning?"

"Twenty-five yards," came the muffled answer.

"Where did you hit 'em?"

"I center-punched him, Cecil. The arrow went through both lungs."

"Did he go far?"

"About 150 yards."

"Tony said you hit him with your second shot. What happened to the first?"

"I twigged out. I don't know how, but I hit a twig somewhere along the way. The arrow hit a tree right above the bull. You know what? He didn't even flinch. I thought for sure the game was over because that arrow made a loud *crack* when it hit. But he just bugled at us again. Can you believe that? Tony got him to bugle again."

"He must really have been hot."

"Not really, Cecil. He would bugle enough for Tony and me to keep tabs on him, but he wouldn't come in. We had to get in his face before things got interesting. That old boy sure boiled out of there when my arrow smacked into him."

Elbo suddenly grew serious as he looked at the rack of his fourth bow-killed elk. "You guys think it'll make the book?"

I looked over at the massive 6x7 leaning against the stump behind Cecil. "Elbo, I'd be surprised if it doesn't." Cecil and Tony nodded in agreement.

That was the start of a long evening of swapping hunting stories. Cecil's centered around elk and elk hunting. He had some good ones to tell after years of being an outfitter in the mountains north of Pierce, Idaho. Tony was partial to bear hunting stories. Of course, if I woke up in the middle of the night with a sow pulling at the bottom of my sleeping bag and her two cubs digging for something under my pillow, I would pass that information along any chance I could.

Elbo was a little different. He loved to tell hunting stories, but he also enjoyed reliving his days as a drill instructor with the U.S. Marine Corps. Me? I just kept putting logs on the fire so there was enough light to see my notebook. Minnesota whitetails are thrilling game to pursue, but they pale in comparison to bugling bulls and charging bears when sitting around an Idaho campfire.

The story telling ended late that night. It was powerful stuff. Not many things can battle for long the hazy exhaustion that some hunters call "fresh-air poisoning."

Hunting stories. They are the lifeline of our sport. Every North American Hunting Club member has tales to tell whether he has hunted Alaska or his own Back 40.

Why are hunting stories told? There are a number of reasons. They are fun to tell—and to hear. We use them to pass on hunting traditions. To teach. To share. They allow us to brag without really bragging. They are harmless—they are dangerous. They are also great ice-breakers.

NAHC Chairman of the Board Paul Burke makes a habit of stopping by the offices of new employees of the NAHC and welcoming them to the club. I was fresh out of college when Paul stopped by my office, and more than a little nervous about meeting the head of the organization. Paul came in, shook my hand, and said, "Mark LaBarbera tells me you like to hunt. Ever hunted bear?" When I admitted that I hadn't, he motioned for me to sit down. "Steve," he began, "I follow two rules when I hunt bears, especially the brown and the griz."

I immediately loosened up. I expected to get a dose of do's and don'ts for the corporate world, instead the chairman of the board was telling the do's and don'ts of bear hunting.

"My first rule is: Don't underestimate the killing power of a bear. My second rule is: Don't attempt to face a charging brown bear when armpit deep in a swampy sinkhole."

I understood Paul's first rule, but his second had me a little baffled and it showed. Paul laughed, knowing full well he had an opportunity to tell another hunting tale.

"Steve, a number of years ago I hunted with a friend, Dick Spurzem, for moose and brown bear on the Alaskan Peninsula, about 125 miles out from King Salmon. Things didn't go too well at first. The outfitter didn't have enough guides for everyone and was lazy to boot. One night he just pulled the boat up on shore and left it there."

"What's wrong with that," I asked.

"The tides cause a lot of problems," he answered. "The next morning we woke up and found the motor full of sand and salt water. It took us a lot of time to get it started after that and once almost cost us our lives."

"What? What happened?"

"I'll tell you in a little bit."

"About a week into the hunt the outfitter transferred me and the guide to a spike camp on the far side of the peninsula. I really shouldn't call it a 'spike camp' because all it was, was a two-man tent and nothing else. My guide, Bud, it turned out, was probably the very best guide I have ever had on a hunt. He was around 40 years old and trapped in Alaska about five months out of the year.

He sure knew how to read sign and weather conditions. One time we heard some wolves howling during the day and Bud turned to me and said, 'That's bad.' When I asked him why, he told me that howling wolves during the day means bad weather is moving in."

"Did it?" I asked him.

"Boy did it," he answered with a chuckle. "A storm rolled in from the Pacific and we spent the next two days holding down the tent. It was blowing so hard at times that the guy sleeping on the wind-blown side of the tent had nylon in his face all night while the other guy had a balloon above him. We were using one of those Coleman Prairie Schooner tents that uses fiberglass poles and looks like an old prairie schooner wagon without the wagon. Any other kind of tent would have been ripped to shreds."

"It's odd that you didn't get any rain."

"But we did. The storm dumped so much water on us during that two-day period that all the nearby streams went from knee-deep to shoulder-deep for the rest of our stay. We couldn't safely cross most of them, so we were limited to hunting close to camp. That hurt. A number of times we spotted nice brown bears, but were unable to go after them on account of the swollen streams."

"Why didn't you head back to the base camp?"

"We did later, but there was only one day left in our hunt by the time we got back."

"Were there any brownies near the base camp?"

"Yea, the outfitter mentioned that he had spotted three bears in a huge swamp directly behind the camp, so Bud and I got up early the next day to try for one of them. We probably should have stayed in bed."

"Why?"

"The motor on the rubber raft took so long to start. Bud pulled on that thing at least 80 times before he gave up. I spelled him a bit and finally got it started about 20 yanks later. Looking back, I kind of wish the thing never started because of what happened later."

I fell for it. "What happened later?"

"I'll let you know in a minute."

"We finally left camp and headed across the bay, which was about five miles across. We entered a river and followed it another seven or eight miles. The trouble was, the farther upriver we went, the shallower it got. We kept running into sand bars all the time. We finally hit one hard enough that the motor konked out—and we couldn't restart it."

"Why didn't you just walk after that? If the river was that low there had to be an exposed shoreline that was easy to follow."

"There was, so we did get out and walk. Bud said that we were only two or three miles from the spot the outfitter told us he had spotted the bears earlier.

"Now before I continue, I want to mention that I told Bud not to shoot at a brown bear unless I was in imminent danger of being mauled or killed. I didn't go all the way to Alaska to watch some trigger-happy guide shoot a brown bear for me.

"When we got to the swamp, Bud took the lead and started to cross it. It wasn't 20 minutes later that he stopped, pointed at something ahead of us and said, 'Here comes a brown bear running right at us—get up next to me and get ready to shoot.' That's when I made a big mistake. In my attempt to hurry, I took a little shortcut across an area with no grass growing in it. Do you know what that means?"

"Yea, you got wet," I answered with a chuckle. "There was no grass growing there because the water was too deep for it to grow."

"Exactly."

"How deep was it?"

"Don't know for sure. I went in to my armpits before I grabbed a clump of swamp grass and pulled myself out. When I finally spotted the bear, he was only 90 yards away and coming fast.

"I knelt down next to Bud and quickly put the crosshairs on him. The bear looked huge in the scope! All I could see was his head and part of his shoulder. Bud whispered, 'Shoot him now.'

"I wanted to take him where the neck meets the shoulder, but the bear was weaving his head from side to side as he ran and the bullet hit the bear a little under his right eye. He went down like a ton of bricks."

"I bet that was a relief!"

"Oh, it was—until he got back up!"

"He got back up? What caliber were you shooting?"

"A .338 Winchester Magnum."

"A .338? How could anything get up after taking a hit in the head from that?"

"What happened, I found out later, was that the bullet was deflected by his skull and went down his windpipe and out his chest—it didn't hit anything vital!"

"What happened then?"

"I shot again, and this time I hit him in the shoulder. He went down again and rolled over. I remember seeing all four feet straight up in the air."

"He was finally down for good, huh?"

"Hardly."

"You've got to be kidding?"

"No, he got up again, only this time he figured he had enough of us and started to stagger off to our right. Bud shouted, 'Shoot him again and kill him quick because I don't want to have to skin him in the creek!' I shot him again in the chest, but it was too late. He crawled into the creek and died."

"How deep was the water?"

"Just over our hip boots."

"I bet it was cold."

"So cold it hurt—and we had to stand in it for over an hour and a half before we finished skinning the bear."

"What time was it when you made it back to the boat?"

"About six."

"What time did it get dark?"

"About 20 minutes later."

"How about the motor? Did you get it restarted?"

"No. We pulled on that rope at least 100 times and it didn't even cough. Bud even disassembled the magneto and checked the spark plugs but nothing helped."

"What did you do?"

"That's exactly what I asked Bud. 'What do we do now?' You know what he answered?"

"No. What?"

"He said, 'We are going to stay active or get hypothermia and die. We are also going to keep this boat in the middle of this here river.' "

"Why did he say that?"

"Because there was a good chance that we would run into a bear on the way back and we didn't want him to get the jump on us in the dark.

"We shoved off and started paddling downriver. The current helped a lot. I was a little surprised how fast we made it back to the bay."

"I bet that was a relief."

"It was—at first. About a third of the way across, we hit some dense fog. It was so thick that we couldn't see 15 or 20 feet ahead of us. All the while we could hear the ocean breaking against the point of land where our base camp was located. I started to get concerned so I asked Bud what would happen if we couldn't make it to shore in time to hit the point. You know what he said?''

''What?''

''We were on our way to Japan!''

''You obviously made it.''

''Yea, but it wasn't easy. Have you ever tried to paddle one of those rubber rafts?'' I nodded in agreement. ''Then you know how difficult they are to move. I didn't have much strength left when we finally hit the beach about a half mile from camp.''

''That's an incredible story, Mr. Burke,'' I told him as he got up to leave.

Paul just turned and said, ''Welcome aboard, Steve, glad to have met you.''

After Paul left, I sat at my desk for a few minutes and pondered my meeting with the head of the NAHC. Having been a member of the NAHC for some time before I was hired, it suddenly came to me what had just happened.

Paul was showing me the reason the NAHC was formed in the first place. He knew that hunters across North America wanted to share their stories as he had just done. He also knew that, like him, they wanted to hear stories from other hunters so they could learn about what methods are successful for the average guy and avid hunter. They didn't want to be preached to by ''professionals'' who always take record book game and never miss a shot. And they wanted to discover new and better places to hunt.

About then, NAHC President Steve Burke stopped in my office with an extended hand and a cheery ''Congratulations.'' I had met Steve earlier while interviewing for my position, so I expected him to approach me in a business-like way. Instead, he treated me like a friend, a buddy who he had shared a duck blind with for years. Oh, he explained the important things about the office; where to go for what, who runs which department and where the coffee machine was located, but he also asked me if I liked to hunt whitetail deer. When I told him that I spent so much time bowhunting during my college days that my grades suffered irreparable damage, he just chuckled a little and said, ''Good, then you'll appreciate this story.''

''You know the club has land leased in a number of states around the country?''

''Sure,'' I answered.

''Well, a few years ago I was hunting one of the leases with

Mark LaBarbera, Paul, Russ Nolan and NAHC members Delbert Ward, Dan Buss and Scott Ekenberg. Hunting wasn't that great the first day, but Russ shot a nice six-pointer on the second. The big story in camp that night was the huge buck Scott heard snorting and stomping just out of sight of his stand that evening.

"Now, I knew about this buck. I had spotted him a couple of years back. But I didn't hunt him that day because I had wasted my two previous seasons on him and never got a shot. I let Scott use my stand in the big buck's area with the hope that Scott's luck would be better than mine. That's how the buck earned the name 'Scott's Buck.'

"The next weekend we returned for the second weekend of the deer season. Unfortunately, Scott had to work that weekend and wouldn't be able to hunt again for the rest of the year. I reclaimed my stand."

"Where was it located? I mean, what kind of terrain was it in?" I asked before he continued.

"It was on the edge of a grassy meadow. The buck never actually ventured into the open, but often used a trail that lead through the thick brush near it.

"Before I forget, I want to mention that another NAHC member, Mike Pointe, came up to hunt with us. Mike was lucky in the antlerless drawing and was still looking for his first deer, so I put him in an area that was known for large numbers of deer, but rarely was frequented by truly huge bucks.

"Hunting was pretty slow on the first day. But things picked up on the second. About 8:00 I heard a rifle shot in the distance. I knew it had to be one of our hunting party because there were no other hunters in the area. I was going to head in the direction of the shot, but decided against it figuring that if somebody needed help field dressing an animal or dragging one out they could come and get me because everyone knew how to find everyone else.

"About an hour later, I heard someone coming to get me. At least, that was what I thought at first. A couple seconds later, I knew it was deer, not hunters, approaching. I spotted the buck first and then the doe. It was Scott's Buck!"

"How far away was he?"

"At that time about 100 yards, but he was heading right toward me at a fast walk."

"Was he spooked?"

"I think so because both of them kept turning around and staring at something behind them."

"I bet it was easy to get your gun up without being seen."

"No trouble at all. I just got into shooting position and found him in my scope. I pulled the trigger when he entered an opening about 50 yards away."

"Did he drop right away?"

"In his tracks."

"What gun were you shooting?"

"I have a Browning BBR .30-06."

"How big was he?"

"A ten-pointer."

"That's bigger than anything I've shot so far."

"It's still my best."

"By the way, did you ever find out who fired the other shot?"

"Yea, it was member Mike Pointe. He had taken a nice seven-point that tried to sneak past his stand shortly after the sun came up. It was his first deer.

"Well, Steve, I just stopped by to say hi and ease you into your first day. Good luck. If you have any questions, just ask."

That was my introduction to the real camaraderie of the North American Hunting Club. You can imagine how comfortable that made my first day at the new job. You know how it is when you're in a new situation with people you haven't previously met. It can be awkward, especially if there's nothing worthwhile to talk about.

But the minute you discover one of the others is a hunter, then it's a different story. There's an instant comfort level and friendship. You can identify with someone who has experienced the thrill that comes when, after hours of waiting, a trophy whitetail heads down the trail you're watching. You can relate to his pride when he tells stories of his young setter pup's first point. As non-hunters in the group look on, you're the only one who can understand what he means when he talks about satisfaction that comes from a sore shoulder at the end of a long day of shooting.

And he listens with understanding when you revel in the successful recollections of *your* last hunt.

Half the fun of hunting adventures is experiencing them. The other half comes from sharing them. Sometimes, maybe more than half of the pleasure comes from reliving the adventure.

As North American Hunting Club members, we all enjoy a good adventure. And the next best thing to hearing a good hunting tale, is reading one.

That's why we pulled together 43 of the best hunting stories we've ever read. They are all true stories, told by North American

Hunting Club members in their own words. These men and women are not writers. They are farmers, students, doctors, housewives, laborers, morticians, executives and mechanics. They are like you and me. We share a common bond—we all love hunting and we all love to swap hunting stories.

We hope you enjoy them as much as we enjoyed pulling them together for you. Maybe next time your hunting tales will fill these pages.

1

Brown Bear At 26 Paces

by Alden Glidden

"Shoot," whispered my guide Kelly.

His words went unheard. In my focused concentration, no sound registered in my brain. It didn't matter. No one had to tell me to shoot as the lumbering giant of a brown bear came straight at me from 30 yards away.

Having grown up on a small farm in Michigan, I was limited in my hunting to what I could accomplish with a 12 gauge single. But after my chores were finished in the evening, my dreams were not limited. I could fantasize while reading *Field & Stream*. One small ad for brown bear hunting on Kodiak Island, picturing three huge bear hides stretched against the side of an old, weathered barn stimulated my wildest dreams and aspirations. When I read the book *The Last Of The Great Brown Bear Men* by Marvin Clark some 30 years later, I recognized the same photo. When I read that the two great guides, Bill Pinnell and Morris Talifson, were still going strong, I decided that I was going to realize the dream of my youth. I was going bear hunting!

Bill responded to my letter in November of 1984. They had one opening for April of 1986, and my deposit went out in the next mail. I then invested in a .340 Weatherby Magnum and plenty of practice. I sighted my rifle in using 250-grain ammo at 200 yards. The distance, as I was to learn, was unduly optimistic.

As the Grumman Goose flew south from Kodiak, all we could

see were the snow covered mountains of the barren island. Only as we approached the southern aspect did the snow fields break up revealing a brown, treeless terrain. We soon circled above the Olga Bay Cannery where Bill and Morris have lived and headquartered their hunting operation since 1941.

At the dock, we were met by the smiling figure of 88-year-old Bill Pinnell; 76-year-old Morris Talifson hustled me into their office to sign my license, then out to the shooting range for a last minute check. Another short flight in the Goose had us back into Karluk Lake where I would be hunting. Joe Bartnicki from Old Forge, Pennsylvania was the second hunter going to Karluk. Our two guides were Jeff and Kelly Hirsch, two brothers originally from Choteau, Montana. Kelly had previously worked for Pinnell and Talifson as a packer, but this was to be his first year as an assistant guide and I was to be his first hunter.

Winter had yet to leave Karluk, rendering the boats useless. This meant our hunting was limited by the amount we wanted to walk. Frigid winds and intermittent snow continued and spotting of bears was sparse. The few seen were badly rubbed.

Kelly and I spent the entire fifth day of the hunt glassing Canyon Creek Canyon without seeing a bear. We arrived at camp by dark, greeted by Bill who had spent the day with camp chores. We finally gave up on Joe and Jeff making it back that evening. We ate and went to bed. We were awakened shortly after 3:00 a.m. by their return. They had found an unrubbed bear, and Joe took it with a successful running shot at dusk. They skinned out the bear and struggled back to camp under the load guided only by their flashlights. Morning revealed a beautiful dark chocolate-colored barren sow which squared at eight feet.

The weather was clear and cold. We returned to Canyon Creek and a knoll where we could glass the snowfields a mile away. By late morning we still had not seen any game. We moved high up onto the south slope where we traversed the snowfields into the canyon at a high enough altitude so that our scent wouldn't be carried into the valley below. The snow was unpredictable, and each step meant the possibility of sinking to the tops of our hip boots.

As noon passed, we crossed over the top of the ridge to glass further down the canyon. As we climbed higher the wind was nearly blowing us off the mountain and it was a relief to drop over the ridge onto the sheltered side to break for lunch.

That's where we first spotted him. Even at a half mile, he

looked bulky and cumbersome. He appeared dark brown with lighter shoulder patches that at a distance we couldn't determine as rubbed areas or a color variation. After some intent study, Kelly said, ''He's a good one!'' The bruin was three-quarters of the way up the other side of the canyon, but seemed to be moving downhill. While we watched, the wind picked up and it began to snow.

In watching him move down to the canyon floor we determined that the light patches were small symmetrical rubs, but that he was big! We hadn't been seeing many bear, so despite the rubs, I decided I wanted to try for him.

It looked like he was going to meander up our side of the canyon, so we hurriedly headed down the slope to a small clear patch, being careful to stay downwind. The crust refused to hold, so with each step we sank to the tops of our hippers. We were anything but quiet, but Kelly assured me that we wouldn't spook him. In fact, he said, a bear just out of the den would probably come to investigate noise!

At our designated clearing, we found the visibility was very limited. Knowing the bear had heard us and was headed up the slope, we waited anxiously. It seemed forever before we thought we heard him working his way up through the thick alders, but in the gusting wind we couldn't be sure.

We finally spotted a vague, dark shape sneaking slowly through the alders. He was still upwind, but had gotten above us and was trying to circle downwind from the noise he had heard.

I got ready as Kelly started breaking sticks and making a racket in hopes the bruin would move right in to investigate. Instead he stayed in the alders all the way to our small clearing. Then slowly he began to work his way in our direction.

We quickly decided that I would go down through an alder thicket on the other side of a small ditch out into another clearing where maybe I could get a clear shot. Kelly would follow, but come out further down the clearing.

The brownie spotted the movement the moment I left the thicket. He came to investigate at full throttle! He dropped into a shallow gully as he plowed out of the brush at full speed, then came up the near side with his head held high looking for the intruder, giving me my first clear shot.

The roar of the Weatherby brought silence as he dropped immediately. His huge head (he later scored 26⅞) disappeared into the frozen snow only 26 yards away. We stood there waiting for any signs of life, but the monarch was down for good. The hunt was over.

2

Snowbound Buck

by Rodger E. Warwick

I was wet and cold as I cautiously looked over the crest of the little rise which hid me from the small herd of antelope I'd first seen nearly an hour earlier. The does and fawns were feeding quietly on the far side of a shallow draw about 150 yards away but there was no sign of the buck which had been with them. As I watched them through my binoculars I saw the back of an antelope move into my field of view. Its head was down as it fed along but I had a feeling it was the buck. I had to be sure before I shot, however, and I continued to watch. Finally, the animal lifted its head and I got a good look at it for the first time. It was the buck I had seen earlier.

I had time to study his horns carefully and I saw that they were heavy enough but not quite as long as I had guessed. He was still a fine buck and with the snow not scheduled to let up for several days, I decided to take him. I eased my rifle over the day pack I always try to use as a rest and settled into a solid prone position. Before I could shoot, the buck walked back into the bottom of the draw and out of sight. The does and fawns continued to feed peacefully and all I could do was wait. I began to wonder how I happened to be hunting antelope in five inches of fresh snow with more falling by the minute.

My hunt had begun some eight months earlier when I had received Wyoming's nonresident license application booklet in the mail. From my home in Billings, Montana, I began planning a late September antelope hunt along with good friend, Doug Dreeszen, also of Billings. Since we had both hunted the area before, we chose Area 74 in central Wyoming. We submitted our applications prior to the March 15th deadline and then had to await the results of the drawing which would assign licenses to the lucky hunters for the coming season.

At nearly the same time as the license application had arrived I had begun looking covetously at a beautiful little Winchester Model 70 XTR Featherweight 7mm Mauser in a local sporting goods store. When we decided on the antelope trip, I went over and put the rifle on lay away. By June it would be mine and I would have the summer to practice and fine tune the rifle before the hunt. Everything went according to plan, and I got the gun in early June and had a local gunsmith install a new Leupold Vari X II 2-7x variable scope with a dot reticle on fine crosshairs.

The rifle performed beyond my expectations and with Federal 140-grain factory ammunition I shot a ⅜-inch three-shot group at 100 yards during the sighting in process. When my permit arrived in the mail during early August I felt I was ready. Unfortunately, Doug did not draw a permit, forcing me to hunt alone. I made a few long distance phone calls and secured permission to hunt. Commitments at work made a September hunt impossible, so I planned my hunt for the first weekend of October.

After a beautiful summer, the regional weather began to deteriorate in late September and unseasonable cold and snow moved in. As I left Billings, Montana, for the 300 mile drive to Casper, Wyoming, it was half raining-half snowing and a cold wind was blowing. Weather reports told me more snow awaited me in my hunting area. It rained or snowed the whole length of my trip and just north of Casper I hit 18 miles of very dense fog. Not exactly the best antelope hunting weather.

The snow got deeper as I drove west of Casper toward my hunting area. The paved roads were still in good condition but the dirt roads looked very questionable. I finally reached my turn off and noticed only one truck track in the snow which covered the little road. As there are several ranches in the area, I was surprised there weren't more. I soon found out why.

With my Ford Bronco in four wheel drive and low range, it took me one hour and 35 minutes to cover the 10 miles to ranch headquarters. The road was in terrible condition from all the moisture the area had received. Even though the road was graveled

it was still nearly impassable. When I reached the ranch and knocked on the door, a startled ranch manager asked, "How in the hell did you get here?" He quickly gave me permission to hunt anywhere I could walk since traveling the ranch trails was out of the question. I thanked him and set out.

Within half a mile I spotted the first antelope I'd seen since leaving Casper. Visibility was terrible and I was quite close before I saw the herd. Their sight was better than mine and they were all staring at me as I tried to locate any bucks in the bunch. They were gone before I could find any.

Shortly after that, I located the small herd mentioned at the beginning of this story. The snow had let up quite a bit and I could see fairly well. I planned a stalk using what cover was available and started toward the herd. By walking and finally crawling I closed the distance, finally getting close enough for a good look. As I lay in the wet snow waiting for the buck to reappear, one of the does began looking intently in my direction. I knew I must have made some small movement which she had seen, but hoped she would calm down. Instead, she turned and began running to my left and slightly away from me. The other does and fawns followed, but the buck still did not come out of the draw. Finally, I saw black horns against the snow as the buck raced to catch up with the departing herd. When he came out of the draw he was really running and my only opportunity was a 200-yard running shot. I swung well in front of the buck's nose and pulled the trigger. He went down in a flurry of snow but was up again just as quickly as he had fallen. He was out of sight before I could shoot again.

I ran to the top of a nearby hill and located the does and fawns still running south as they had started but there was no sign of the buck. Thinking he might have fallen again, I began tracking him in the snow. I found where he had fallen and saw two small spots of blood in the snow. He had turned west into broken country after he had gone out of my sight and I began following as fast as I could.

Three ridges later, I caught up with the buck in a huge flat area several hundred yards across. He was a long way off, walking slowly to my left. I got into a good prone shooting position with my pack on top of a piece of sage brush and rested my rifle on top of the pack. When the buck stopped walking I held carefully on his shoulder and shot. He showed no reaction at all. I quickly shot again with the same lack of results. Three shots later, I still had not even gotten his attention. Frustrated, I reloaded and started all over again. I looked at the buck once more and it suddenly dawned on me that he was much farther away than I had originally thought. I settled back behind the rifle and held the dot above his back line with the vertical crosshair just even with his front leg. At the shot the buck took one step and fell into the snow.

I stood and gathered my gear and began the walk out to where the buck lay. I counted 378 long paces to the buck. That is much farther than I like to shoot and I wouldn't have tried it if the animal had not been hit earlier. Since I'd seen no blood while trailing the buck other than the two spots where he had fallen, I was most interested in seeing where he had been hit by my first shot. The bullet had gone through the bridge of his nose below and in front of the eyes and made a pencil hole which had bled very little. My lead had been too great on the running shot.

I was very glad to finally get the buck since I had been experiencing that sick feeling in the pit of my stomach which every hunter knows when it seems as though a wounded animal may get away to suffer needlessly.

3

President's Trophy Winner

A Mexican Cliffhanger
by Robert Miller

I waited 31 years for my first sheep hunt. The result was a good curl and a quarter Dall sheep from Canada's Northwest Territories. Five years later I was in Mexico looking for the rarest of North America's big game trophies, the desert bighorn. The result of that hunt was a new Safari Club world record desert sheep and the Number Five Boone and Crockett desert bighorn. The kind of trophy every big game hunter dreams about.

After two days of flying, I was finally in the shotgun seat of a 4x4 pickup heading south of Baja, California, toward the Sun Matias Mountains. Guadalupe (Lupe) was driving the 4x4, Rafael sat between us.

Before the trip to the mountains started, George Bello, the outfitter, instructed me that Lupe would be the chief guide, Rafael the camp chief. Together we would drive to our base camp, La Palmita, about 200 miles south of Mexicali.

After hours of bouncing over hot dirt roads, we arrived in base camp at dusk. The Spanish-English translator who was supposed to accompany us on the hunt had taken ill and was not able to come. None of us in the hunting party could speak Spanish and no one thought of bringing a Spanish-English dictionary. We had been advised prior to the trip that each hunter would have a translator.

In base camp I met Cuauhtemoc and Jose, the spotters, Mario and Francisco, the packers, Reyna the cook, and Adolfo, the camp guard. I noted the location of the cook tent, the sleeping tents, the latrine and the bottled water.

The fun began when we tried to discuss what was going to happen in the days ahead. I learned very quickly that we had a total communication gap, but promised myself I would not allow this to interfere with the hunt.

After a long sleepless night, and burritos for breakfast, I sighted in my rifle and followed my guides up the mountain in search of the second sheep towards a Grand Slam.

Everyone except Adolfo, the camp guard, climbed aboard the two pickups. We headed farther south and higher into the mountains. Three hours later we came to a stop at the north end of a ravine and unloaded the trucks. Rafael and Reyna began setting up a small outcamp while Lupe and I again went through the process of deciding what should be left at this camp and what should be taken into the mountains. The rest of the men began shouldering backpacks and sleeping bags. I was told by elementary hand signals, that we would depart immediately and spend two or three days hunting in the surrounding mountains. If we were unsuccessful, we would return to this camp, then move on to another where we would spend an additional two or three days. This process would continue during the 10-day hunt, or until we were successful in taking a ram.

The first day was fruitless and, in more ways than one, you might say we came up dry. I heard plenty of tales about a giant ram—*Borrego Grande*—that haunted these high mountains, but all we saw that first day were two ewes and three kids.

The next morning I awakened to the crackling of a fire. As I crawled from my sleeping bag and began to get dressed, I could see that Lupe and Cuauhtemoc had finished breakfast and were beginning to pack up for the day's hunt. I started moving faster when I learned they were going to start up the mountain without me so they could start glassing for sheep at the break of day. I, along with everyone else in camp, was to follow as soon as I had finished breakfast. This discouraged me for three reasons: 1. I had never hunted where the guides went ahead and began glassing before the hunter. 2. I wanted to be able to discuss and plan the events of the day. 3. They were climbing the same mountain we had climbed the day before.

During breakfast, hot chili burritos, I began to notice the aches and pains that had been caused by the previous day's activities. Later that morning, on top of the mountain, I began to wonder if I

NAHC member Robert Miller, right, shakes hands with one of the guides that led him to a world record desert bighorn in the Sun Matias Mountains

had trained and conditioned enough. I took off my hiking shoes to discover blisters the size of half dollars on the inside of each heel. Even though the blisters were considered humorous by my friends, I could tell they were concerned. If you can't keep your feet in good health on a backpack sheep hunt, you are in big trouble.

Once on top, I was rewarded with a spectacular view in every direction. There was only one peak higher than the one we were on. It lay across a large saddle to our southeast. We walked across a little flat area of the mountain to a sheer cliff which dropped straight down for several thousand feet. From this vantage point we could see the valleys below to the east, the plateaus beneath us to the north and around to the south, and across the saddle and up the peak to the southeast.

We had glassed for only a short time when Lupe sent Cuauhtemoc across the saddle and up the peak to the southeast. The rest of us kept glassing in all directions. We would periodically glass the peak Cuauhtemoc was climbing. I was sitting with Lupe when he glassed where Cuauhtemoc had gone and I saw emotion burst across his face. When I swung my glasses toward the peak, I could see Cuauhtemoc crouched down, motioning for us to come. In any language worldwide, that signal ignites the adrenaline in a hunter's body.

At a full trot, we went down the slope, across the saddle and up the peak toward Cuauhtemoc. The pace slowed to a fast climb when we started up the mountain.

Everyone was on the peak now except Francisco. He had departed at the last glassing area, to go back to the outcamp, where Rafael and Reyna were staying, to pick up food and water. We were a day and a half from the outcamp. If we went down the other side of the mountain we would be two days away, and we only had one day's supply of food. Francisco would return with enough supplies for two more days for each of us.

As we approached, I could see the emotion in Cuauhtemoc's eyes. He and Lupe were deep in discussion while the head guide was setting up the spotting scope. They would climb back to the vantage point where Cuauhtemoc had seen the ram. Jose, Mario and myself were to stay on this side of the mountain, which would reduce the chance for the ram to see, hear or wind us.

When they got into position Lupe looked through the glass, then quickly turned around and motioned for me to stay low and climb up. I made my way to Lupe's position with my rifle on my back, crawling on my hands and knees the last few yards. Lupe signaled for me to take off my hat and move up to the scope very carefully, take a short look and return. When I looked through the scope, my heart fluttered. Although the ram was a mile away and mirage made the scene ripple, I saw immediately we had found *Borrego Grande*.

Lupe and Cuauhtemoc were as excited as I. They made plans while I tried to keep my heart inside my shirt. Lupe instructed Mario to go back to the last glassing area and wait for Francisco.

From this point onward, not a word was spoken in any language. They had decided that we would move one at a time, southward along the west side of the ridge, keeping the ram on the east. The wind was blowing from west to east, therefore we would have to go high on the mountain and hope the wind would blow our scent over the sheep and not down onto the plateau where he was grazing.

We had to move quickly, quietly and cautiously in treacherous terrain. Lupe led the way. He literally ran, jumping from rock to rock, going upwards along the west side of the ridge. He went for about 100 yards, crawled up to the peak of the ridge, and checked to see that the ram was still there. Lupe then crawled back down and motioned for Cuauhtemoc. The same procedure was used to traverse an entire mile.

Suddenly, Lupe came to the end of the mountain, a sheer cliff. He could go no further. He motioned for Cuauhtemoc and me to come ahead and join him, then crawled to the peak of the mountain to observe the location of our quarry. The sheep was still there and not aware of our presence. Lupe sent Cuauhtemoc down the west side of the mountain to see if there was any way we could get around the sheer cliff. I stayed in position while Cuauhtemoc left and Lupe crawled back to the top to keep the ram in view. Cuauhtemoc returned in about 40 minutes. There was no alternate route. Lupe indicated he wanted me to join him at the peak of the mountain. I crawled back up to the crest, then the two of us made our way to a little rock ledge on the sheep's side, keeping our silhouettes from being skylined. Lupe and I made ourselves as comfortable as possible, clinging to that 24-inch ledge.

We were as far as we could go now, and I was totally exhausted. My heart was pounding like a two-cylinder engine, and my lungs were gasping like a pulsating bellows. Lupe set up the spotting scope while I tried to regain my composure. With the naked eye I could tell it was a sheep, but I couldn't tell if it had horns. With the field glasses there was no doubt; this was the male species of *Ovis canadensis nelsoni*. I estimated the range at 700 yards.

I was sitting to Lupe's left, and when he put his right eye to the spotting scope, his left eye translated the excitement I wanted to see.

He pulled back from the scope slowly and indicated that I should take a look. When I lowered my right eye to the 35X lens, my first impression was that the scope was filled with one pair of horns. I don't recall seeing any other part of the animal.

I looked down quickly at my left hand, which was braced on a rock to keep me from falling off the ledge. Blood was flowing out between my fingers and my fingernails. When I had been southbound on the west side of the mountain, I was using my left hand as a brace to keep from falling off the cliffs. I was so caught up in the excitement of this stalk that I hadn't noticed I had worn three of my fingers raw. Luckily, I'm a right handed shooter and my right hand was OK.

Bleeding fingers weren't my only problem though. I was at the end of my mountain world and the sheep was still 700 yards away. He was about 200 yards south and 500 yards straight down.

Lupe asked if I could shoot that far. I shook my head no. He then asked me at what distance I would feel comfortable shooting. I held up one finger and made a bull's-eye. I held up two fingers and made a bull's-eye. I held up three fingers and made a shaky bull's-eye. I held up four fingers and made a shakier bull's-eye. I held up five fingers and motioned that I didn't know. I held up six fingers and shook my head no. I held up seven fingers and shook my head positively no.

Lupe indicated he wanted me to shoot. I responded with ''Why?'' We were both perplexed at this point, and the communication gap was magnified. To me, our options continued to graze on the little plateau. We would stay where we were, even if it included sleeping overnight. If the ram moved away, not knowing of our presence, we could go back along the ridge, down the mountainside and around its base to see if we could get closer. If the ram moved toward us, he would hopefully come within range and I could put my shooting skill to the test. At this point the ram laid down, keeping his head high and observing all around him.

A bit of demoralization came over me. My body was tired and my throat parched. The ledge was too small for me to move to a more restful position. My water and the rest of my gear had been left with Jose. Lupe again was encouraging me to shoot. He speculated that if I missed, the ram might run up the mountain toward us, offering me a closer opportunity. I respectfully declined, having no intentions of shooting at that distance.

I began preparing myself psychologically to sleep on the mountain, but then *Borrego Grande* stood up. He gazed slowly in all directions, then suddenly started walking more briskly straight towards us, looking back over his right shoulder, as if there was danger in that direction. He came 200 yards closer, now about 500 yards away, then began grazing again.

With more forcefulness and a great sense of urgency, Lupe

urged me to shoot. I pulled my rifle up alongside me, put my camouflage hat on a rock, and laid the rifle on top of the hat. From a prone position on the ledge, I brought the crosshairs to the front shoulder of the ram. *Borrego* was in the shade of a setting sun, but standing in full view. I pulled my eye away from the scope, checked to insure that it was on 9X, and laid my rifle on its side. I looked toward Lupe and indicated that it was too far for me to shoot with any degree of accuracy. Lupe dropped his head as if to say, "What am I going to do with this gringo?"

When I looked back down at the ram, he had begun to move again. But this time not in our direction. He was moving away from us, to our left. Instinctively, I knew it was now or never. Knowing I would have to shoot 500 yards, practically straight down the mountainside, I edged my body forward and to the left so I would have a better vantage point for the shot. I was precariously braced on the rock where my hat and rifle were laying.

Lupe crawled alongside me and grasped my belt and trousers to keep me from falling from the ledge when I fired. I welcomed the feeling of security. I eased the rifle forward and pointed the barrel down the mountain. It was getting dark.

As the sheep appeared in the bottom of the scope, perspiration dropped from my brow and onto the lens. The ram stopped and was motionless, holding his head high, looking over his left shoulder. The perspiration had landed in a quadrant of the lens that did not interfere with my view of the ram. At 500 yards, he occupied a very small portion in the center of the 9X scope. I leveled the crosshairs slightly above his front shoulder.

Immediately after the rifle cracked, I could hear the thud of the 180-grain soft point as it hit home.

The ram dropped, but was up before I could relocate him in the scope. I chambered another cartridge and squeezed again while he was running tangent to our position under a full head of steam. I heard this one ricochet off the rocks beneath him. I chambered my third cartridge and located him in the scope. He was standing motionless, looking in our direction. I took my time positioning the crosshairs.

When the rifle jumped, it was so dark I saw fire spew from the end of the barrel. When I heard the bullet make contact, I knew it was a solid hit. The ram went down. Lupe hollered and hit me on the shoulder so hard I thought he was going to knock me from the ledge.

When I chambered the fourth cartridge Lupe indicated there

was no reason to fire again. When I located him in the scope, I saw he was motionless on the rocks where he had stood. We both jumped to our feet and came alive with our echoing voices.

We had to go back along the crest several hundred yards before we could find a way around the sheer cliff to the ram. The others had started down the mountain independently of each other, but we could see their individual locations on the mountainside. Soon, it was so dark they had to use flashlights.

It took us an hour to descend the mountain. We were the last ones to get there, except Mario and Francisco. We could see their flashlights half way down the mountain. A fire was built to help Mario and Francisco locate our exact position. Lupe and I went directly to the ram.

There was no mistaking that the ram would rank high in the record books. An inspection of his mouth revealed only one tooth in his bottom jaw. A hasty measurement of the horns indicated that both were over 40 inches and both bases were close to 15 inches. We were ecstatic.

While eating dinner, I tried to explain that we were not going to skin the ram that night. I wanted to wait until morning to take photographs. Dinner and sleep were very welcome. The next morning, after the camera session, we skinned the animal for a full mount, broke camp and began the long journey back to the outcamp.

The climb over the first mountain was easy because of the joy that was still rattling around in my head. However, by the time we were half way up the second mountain, the fun had worn off. It was a most difficult trek back to the outcamp, one that took the entire day.

Reyna meticulously fried the backstraps and sweetbreads from the ram. I broke out my supply of Jamaican cigars and Holland brandy and passed them around in celebration.

The following day we drove back to Mexicali. I was introduced to Eliseo Aravjo, who scored my sheep at 188. Later it was scored by the Boone and Crockett Club at 187 and the Safari Club International at 190—SCI's world record desert sheep at the time. Eight months later, a bigger sheep knocked it down to second place in the book. It was the second ram I had taken, but my Number Two is Number One with me.

4

I Think I Shot the Biggest One

by Tom Lillibridge

Three bucks ran out in the open and looked back at the trees beneath me. My first thought was that they had caught my scent or saw me move. Not so. What they were looking at was a coyote trotting along the creek, probably looking for an easy meal. About a hundred yards to the east of these three deer was another buck. This one was a dandy.

This particular scene unfolded a week before the 1986 South Dakota West River deer season was scheduled to open. I was out on a Saturday morning scouting trip in my favorite area just to see what might be available. I don't ever remember seeing four whitetail bucks within a 100 yards of each other, much less three of them that could have been touched with a 10-foot pole. With such promising sign, I could hardly wait until the next weekend.

That area was my favorite hunting area for good reason. I have taken a number of good bucks there including a 9x7 whitetail that won the 1981 NAHC Non-Typical Whitetail Deer award for firearms. My stand, as such, is on a bluff overlooking a heavily wooded creek that has produced one 4x4, two 5x5's and the 9x7 for me over the years, plus the first deer ever for the young son of a friend of mine. That one was a big 6x5.

I got the 9x7 on the second day of the 1980 season. I was sitting on the bluff when I heard the crash of antlers and enough other noises to know that a major battle was taking place. Within a short time, a nice 5x5 came busting out of the woods and ran into the trees beneath me. Hot on his tail was an even bigger buck with a bushy looking rack on his head. The deer made a complete circle back to where they started, then ran the same route again. The third time they ran their circle the five-pointer headed south across the creek and over to the neighbor's farm.

Apparently, the big boy was proud of himself because he went back to the area where the fight had started and proceeded to continue the battle with the trees, bushes, or whatever else was available. Within minutes, two other bucks scattered in different directions; one, a small 2x2, crossed the clearing and walked under my stand. Two or three minutes later, the boss followed the forkhorn across the clearing and into the wooded creek area. After making sure that the competition had left, he turned toward home. Fortunately, he made a stop in an opening and one shot from my Remington .30-06 Woodsmaster Model 742 added him forever to my collection of memories.

In the fall of 1986, I was back in the same spot on the second day of deer season. The weather was terrible the first day. The wind was howling and cold, and at least the deer had been smart enough to stay put on that kind of day. But the second day dawned warm and comfortable. The 1980 season started the same way; lousy weather the first day and nice weather the second. I was on my stand by first light. There were deer all over the place. Several deer came back to the creek bottom from nearby corn fields. Most of them were whitetails, but somebody up the creek scared a small band of mulies into this bottom area. I had never seen whitetails and mule deer square off nose to nose before. The whitetail does were definitely more aggressive, and after a few head butts, the lead doe of the mulie band headed out for more peaceful territory.

The does and fawns were wandering all over the place. So were the bucks. There was a nice four-point, a small forkhorn, a three-pointer whose left horn turned down and went across the front of his face, and two big five-pointers. One of the five-pointers followed a doe over a hill and up the creek. He had a nice heavy rack that wasn't real wide, but looked to be quite tall. The other one walked directly away from me once, and although he was too far away to shoot, I could see the horns extended way out past his ears. That was the one I wanted!

I sat in the same spot from before 7:00 until almost 10:30 and I doubt if a half hour went by without seeing at least one deer. There wasn't any snow on the ground, so it was harder than usual

Tom Lillibridge took this buck on opening day on land he had been hunting for years. Two days later, he bought the property.

to see the deer moving through the trees. A movement directly below me, however, caught my eye. I could see a doe standing in an open area. After looking around for two or three minutes, she proceeded to lie down. It was fun watching her from about 50 yards away through my binoculars and spotting scope. Her attention was definitely concentrated on something, and in trying to follow her gaze I could see what it was. The boss buck—and he was only 50 yards away.

I couldn't shoot immediately. The buck was behind a bushy tree and I couldn't find a place to thread a bullet through. His antlers were visible, though, and I stared in awe through the glasses. It seemed an eternity before he moved a couple of steps to give me an opening. A 150-grain Winchester Power Point from my Remington 742 put him down for good.

The creek between the deer and me was running pretty fast, so after being sure that my trophy wasn't going anywhere I had to take my Scout and drive almost five miles to get back to the other side of the creek. The adrenalin was really flowing as I walked up to the deer and saw how nice he really was. As I looked around the area I realized that less than 25 yards away was the place I shot my 9x7 buck one week short of six years earlier.

There is another buck in the area that was already a big guy last year. I didn't get as close of a look at him as I did the one I shot, but I think I shot the biggest one. Anyway, I plan to be back next year in the same spot to find out.

By the way, the second day of the season was on Sunday, and Monday morning I bought the section of land I have been hunting all these years.

5

A Black Bear With A Brown Bow

by Jay Verzuh

As I sloshed across the driveway, I lifted my eyes to the distant blue line of mountains. It was getting hot and muggy in the low country; time to head for the peaks! The storm that had so rudely delayed my departure for two days finally disembowelled itself, and was now history. Standing in a rapidly disappearing puddle, I looked from the pickup back to the mountains. They were only 20 miles away as the crow flies, but 60 miles and two hours away by truck. I had an appointment up there this evening and I knew I had better get a move on. Maybe this time, Mr. Bear would keep our appointment, and maybe he would even be on time.

Our meeting spot was about 8,500 feet above sea level, in the mountains of Western Colorado. Once again, me and my Brown bow were going looking for a black bear.

There is something special about trying for a bear with a bow, and those of you who have tried it know what I mean. I was hunting over a bait and had two bears working the bait, one small and one that appeared quite large, judging by his tracks. One of them was coming in regularly an hour before dark, which is not real common here in Colorado. I was able to know exactly what time the bear was coming, thanks to my "Trail Timer," a small timing device that every bear hunter should have on every bait.

My tree stand had been up since the day that I first hauled in the bait, so the bears would be accustomed to it. I also had a large burlap bag hanging from a branch above the stand, hopefully conditioning the bear not to spook if he spots some movement by the hunter. I don't know for sure that it helps, but on more than one occasion bears have climbed the tree to check it out. As a matter of fact, it kind of unnerved a lady bowhunter from Texas, one evening, when she found that Mr. Bear had been in her tree stand and left some of his hair behind. She, however, settled down well enough to make a perfect shot on the same bear a few hours later.

During the winding, twisting, climbing drive to my bear stand, I wondered if my "almost" encounter three days prior had ruined my chances to take this bear. Thunderheads had boiled over the horizon shortly before sundown, and along with them came wind gusts from all points of the compass. Shortly thereafter a cow elk with her newborn calf pressed tightly to her flank, burst from the timber below the bait and raced 30 yards into the open park. There she stopped, whirled and blew snot almost back to the timber. Twice more she repeated this scenario before disappearing over the ridge. A tremor went through my body, my pulse quickened, my mouth went dry, and I got ready. My bear was close—only a bear or a lion could make an elk act that way, and I was betting bear. I spent the remaining daylight hours "ready," but he never showed. I had seen a large bear approaching the bait, but it somehow detected me and did not come all the way in. It was nine days before that bait was hit again.

My spirits lifted as I observed a set of bear tracks crossing the road just above the cabin, and only about one half mile from the bait. At least there was still one in the area. I pulled into the cabin and unloaded all my provisions, gear, and extra bait. I planned on spending about a week in the high country—kind of a combination hunt and vacation.

I took the extra bait down by the creek under the cover of the evergreens to keep it from spoiling and stinking. My baiting philosophy employs two general food types. I call them "attractors" and the "main course." The attractors include used cooking grease, bacon grease, molasses and honey. The main course consists entirely of restaurant scraps and butcher shop scraps.

After an early supper, I washed up and changed into my hunting clothes. I pack all of my hunting clothes separately in a large plastic bag to help eliminate any foreign odors from invading the fabric, and possibly alerting Mr. Bear as he comes in.

Remember, we are talking 10 to 15 yards. I discovered years ago that I was not the new Robin Hood, so I overcame my handicap of not being the best archer in the woods by getting very close before I shoot and never taking a marginal shot. If I do not have an unobstructed path to the vitals, I'll wait until I do. This sometimes results in no shot, but that's a lot better than a blood trail with no end.

The truth is, most of the enjoyment and excitement of the hunt is in the moments prior to the release of the arrow or squeeze of the trigger. After that moment, that particular hunt is all over and there will never be another exactly like it.

After dressing, I assembled my bow and gathered up some practice arrows. My "Brown Bow," as I call it, is actually a new Bighorn recurve. This new design featured a heavier riser than my other Bighorn bows and also had a larger sight window, but I felt really comfortable with it and was excited to try it on big game. With the limbs I had on the bow, it pulled about 67 pounds and drew smooth as silk.

After riddling a gopher mound with about a dozen arrows, I climbed up on the porch railing. The porch overlooks the stream bed and is very similar to shooting out of a tree stand. Shooting at a styrofoam cup on the stream bank at about 15 yards, I sent two broadheads in a row through it—time to go hunting.

Finally settling in on my tree stand, I double-checked my safety belt and relaxed. There is absolutely nothing in the world like a June evening in the Colorado mountains.

The sun gently dipped down and the breeze sprung up as if to cue me. Time to stand up and get ready. R and R was over. My senses keyed up and I became aware of everything around me. My brain was totally tuned in to "bear." I slowly nocked an arrow and drew back my bow to loosen my muscles. I had been on stand for two and one half hours. As I reached full draw and held my anchor point for a few seconds, I could still smell bacon on my hands. "Good," I thought, "If I can still smell it, I know Mr. Bear still can." The reason it was so strong was that I had spent the first 20 minutes at the bait burning bacon grease in an old skillet on a single burner gas stove. In that time, I dispersed the aroma from over one half the contents of a three-pound coffee can. This is not one of my common practices, but since the bear had been absent for three days, I thought this might speed up his return.

I slowly let off the bow, then drew once more. I was ready. Everything was perfect. The typical light evening breeze sighed through the pine boughs and cooled my left side. As I stood in my tree stand, I was facing almost due north and the bait was almost directly in front of me. Stretching for a mile behind me was a timbered basin lying above the lip of a very deep canyon. As I looked west, I could see the canyon rim about 80 yards distant. The stand and the bait were located right at the tree line, so I had open country for about 150 yards to the northwest. The bears have always come to this bait from the timbered basin to the south, and generally first come into view between the stand and the canyon rim, about 40 yards from the stand.

I stared at that trail till my eyes crossed, and I heard a bear coming at least a hundred different times. My muscles screamed from immobility. As the shadows lengthened and darkness started capturing the forest, I finally relaxed. After 40 minutes of intense concentration and immobility, my entire body cried out for movement. I took a deep breath and rolled my head around to loosen my neck muscles before climbing down. During the second roll I looked right in the face of a large bear coming over the canyon rim. Walking fast, with his nose in the air, he was headed right for the bait. In a matter of seconds he was there—he never looked left or right—just followed his nose to the bait. It was like the bear had read the script that I had written and rewritten in my mind. As he got to the bait he was perfectly broadside; he stopped and put his head down and away from me, smelling the ground, at the same time moving his front legs forward.

All the aches and tight muscles were gone. It was time for all the hours of practice and experience to pay off, for instinct and reflex to take over. I can remember seeing the yellow and white fletching, like a military tracer bullet, disappear behind the bear's shoulder, causing the damndest ruckus you ever saw.

The bear swung his head around toward the arrow entrance hole, dropped his near shoulder, and did two shoulder rolls directly toward my tree stand. Then he jumped up and ran sideways until he was out of sight over the canyon rim, looking back at the bait the entire time. I heard some rocks roll, then all was quiet; very quiet. I replayed the action in my mind and was convinced that the arrow was good. I felt the shot was right where I wanted it to be.

I carefully climbed down and went to mark the spot where the bear had disappeared from sight, while there was still a hint of light. I stuck an arrow in the ground and turned back toward the bait 80 yards up the hill, I could smell the bacon. It was a good feeling, knowing that it had worked.

As I sat down under my tree stand and prepared to trail the bear an earlier conversation with my wife came to mind. At the time it really hadn't really meant much, but it sure did now. She had made me promise not to trail a bear after dark by myself. After all the nights in the past when I had spent hours crawling around in the brush with a flashlight trailing bears shot by clients, and now I had promised not to do the same for myself??? I'll be honest, I came up with a thousand reasons why I should break the promise, and only one reason not to, and that was trust. Trust won out, and that was the longest night I have ever spent.

Over the past several years as an outfitter, there have been several instances where due to circumstances (poor hit right at dark, etc.) we have had to leave a trail overnight, and I never lost any sleep over it. I knew in my own mind the animal would be at the end of the trail and we would find it, and almost without exception we did. I can remember that those hunters always looked like they hadn't slept a wink that next morning. Well, I found out they hadn't. I didn't either.

In retrospect, I think that was one of the best things that could have happened to me. Maybe over the years, with all the animals, I had misplaced some of the feelings of excitement that go with this great spot. Whatever, they all came back that one night in June. By daylight, I had thought about it and second guessed myself so much that I wasn't sure where that arrow had hit that bear.

At first light I headed for the bait. I drove my ATV right to the arrow sticking in the ground, jumped off, slipped on the frosty grass, and fell right on my backside, a nice way to start the day. I sat there for a minute and had a little chat with myself. I was acting like a greenhorn hunter. It was stupid, but you know what, it was also kind of fun. It was then that I saw the blood spots, splattered all over the grass. I got up and followed the trail over the rim and down the canyon side.

It was all over very shortly, the bear had only run about 40 yards past the arrow before dying. Unfortunately for me, he then rolled about 400 yards and wedged under a dead aspen in the center of a spring, complete with mud and stinging nettles.

It was late afternoon when I made the last trip up the canyon side with the last load of meat, but it was worth every minute, 'cause back at the cabin I got to take some pictures of my Brown Bow with a black bear.

6

One Tough Lion

by John McAteer

When I decided that it was finally time for me to go on the mountain lion hunt I had always dreamed of, I consulted the NAHC's Approved Outfitters & Guides book, read a number of hunting reports submitted by other members and sent out letters to outfitters that I figured could satisfy my itch to take a large lion with archery equipment. Little did I know that one of those letters was going to lead me to one of the largest mountain lion ever taken with a bow and arrow and nomination for the NAHC's President's Award.

After sifting through a number of potential outfitters, I finally booked a hunt with Jerry Boren, who hunts the Bookcliff Mountain Range in Utah. Jerry has a pack of top-notch lion hounds and promised he would try his best to get me a big cat. That was good enough for me.

Our plan was to find a fresh set of lion tracks, let the dogs go and follow them on foot. The plan sounded good, unfortunately, for the first five days of the hunt we couldn't find a fresh set of lion tracks though we investigated over 20 canyons and four or five mountains in that time.

Finally, on February 15, around 7:00 a.m., while riding high on a mountain, we spotted the tracks of a large lion. Jerry immediately let Badger, his best dog, go and directed me to follow him. Jerry said he was going back to the truck to get more dogs. I

quickly shut down my sled and stepped into the three feet of powder, took a deep breath of the thin mountain air and took off after the dog.

The first four miles of the chase were a testimony to my neglected pre-hunt conditioning. The second four almost killed me. I was to the point of total exhaustion when the dogs finally barked "treed." Adrenalin and my love of hunting helped me make it to the bottom of the gorge where the lion was treed 80 feet up in a big pine.

I was mesmerized by the size and beauty of the beast I had traveled so far to hunt. He, in turn, snarled and spit at me while I tried to position myself for the shot. Jerry, meanwhile, was trying to gather the dogs and tie them up out of the way. He didn't want the lion falling on any of them when he came out of the tree.

After carrying my bow over eight miles, I barely had enough strength to draw it back. I finally got the 70-pound Bear compound to break over, aimed and released. The arrow smacked into the lion

NAHC Life Member John McAteer poses with his hard won mountain lion bowkill. The tom scored 15⁷/₁₆, enough to place it Number Five in the Pope & Young record books and qualify it for Boone & Crockett listing.

and seconds later he tumbled out of the tree.

The lion was far larger than either Jerry or I had expected. We caped him out quickly and prepared to head out. Darkness was falling, and we still had an eight-mile walk ahead of us.

The trip out was even worse than I expected. The bitter cold drained what little energy I had left and we got turned around a number of times in the darkness. We finally reached our starting point about 3:00 a.m.—20 hours after we had taken up the lion's tracks.

My lion turned out to be the largest ever taken in the state of Utah. He scored 15%16, qualifying him for the Number Five position in the Pope & Young record book and enough to make Boone and Crockett. A trophy that I will never forget.

7

Carol's Caribou

by Carol Rollings

Approaching the edge of the alders, we could see caribou moving around above us. We moved slowly, now, trying not to alert the herd to our position. They didn't seem to be aware of us at all.

I loaded my rifle as quickly as possible and double checked the safety on my Browning lever action .308. My brother Ed motioned me to move up beside him. He asked if I thought I was up for a 300-yard shot. I looked around for a rest for my rifle, but the tangled alders didn't offer anything for the raised angle I needed.

I just started to tell him that it would be pretty tough when the silence of the valley was broken by the beller of my husband's 7mm Remington Magnum echoing between the mountains. I was happy for Mike when we didn't hear a second shot. I hoped that it meant his dream had come true.

Every whitetail hunter has experienced my next feeling. You know the one you feel when all you see is that white flag bouncing through the brush. All we could see of the trophies that we had been stalking were racks and rumps running up the mountain. We watched them until they topped the ridge and went out of sight. My heart sank to my feet. Ed said, "Well, we came this far, let's see if we can find out where they have gone."

We didn't need to hide anymore so we took off at full speed up the mountain. We were still a long way from the top when weariness forced us to walk, and by the time we reached the point the herd had crossed, the caribou were gone.

We sat down to rest and talk over what to do next. It was still early, so we decided to continue up the mountain. We hoped that we would be lucky and spot the herd casually grazing just over the next rise. "Dream on girl; that's how you got here in the first place," I thought. We continued up the mountain until we found a good spot to look over the valley. Ed and I settled in and started glassing.

Suddenly, I spotted something move across the valley. Ed raised his binoculars to take a closer look. "It's Mike, and he's signaling for us to go to the right," he said.

We cautiously moved further up the mountain. Ed was in the lead and I was right on his heels. Ed suddenly dropped to his knees and told me that he could see several caribou racks just over the hill. We crawled on our bellies for the next 50 yards. Ed raised only his head for a quick occasional look. He reminded me of a prairie dog popping up and down to see what was happening.

I couldn't see anything yet, but Ed indicated the herd's position. We didn't have any cover left, only the slight rise of ground between the caribou and us. Ed slowly rolled up onto his knees and raised his binoculars for a better look. He was careful not to get high enough to see the caribou's eyes, just high enough to judge the racks.

Ed slowly lowered his body, motioned for me to come up to his side. He whispered that the bull second to the rear was the one we were after. "He's the double-shovel with a strand of velvet hanging off the left main beam," Ed said.

I'll admit I felt a bit rushed and more than a little excited.

A cow appeared only 30 yards to my left. She spooked and ran down from us. The rest of the herd followed at a run.

I stood up and raised my rifle. I picked up the bull with the velvet hanging from its beam. He was in the rear of the herd, but his body was blocked by a cow and young bull running beside him.

I heard Ed say, "Shoot, Carol! Shoot!" but I didn't have a clear shot, so I just followed the bull with my rifle scope hoping that he would separate from the herd long enough to put the crosshairs on his shoulder.

The herd disappeared around the hill on which we stood. Ed yelled for me to run, so I ran over the top of the hill to cut them off. Both of us burned rubber to get to the other side. To our disbelief, they were on a dead run less than 60 yards below us. The

herd was spread out a little now. The bull I wanted was trailing the herd by a few yards and running wide open.

"Take him, Sis!!"

It was now or never. I shouldered my rifle, swung the crosshairs past his shoulder and pulled the trigger. The rifle cracked the mountain air like thunder.

As I recovered from the recoil, I watched the bull's front legs fold. His momentum sent his body cartwheeling over his massive rack. Pieces of dirt and lichen were thrown in the air. I'm sure he was dead before his back hit the ground.

My knees started to shake and I started to cry for joy. The bull never moved a hair as we approached him. I was so excited that I didn't even lever another shell.

Ed ran over to me and picked me up and swung me around in circles as he yelled, "You got him Sis! You got him! I didn't think you were ever going to shoot!" All I could do was cry for joy and keep saying, "I did it. I did it!" The two of us just collapsed after the long, hard three-hour stalk. My knees were still shaking too much to stand up.

Two days earlier, Ed had stalked within 60 yards of his double-shoveled trophy to make a beautiful shot with his Ruger Super Blackhawk .44 Magnum pistol. Two double-shovels—first Ed's, then mine—we couldn't believe it. As I looked over at my beautiful caribou, I knew everything we did and planned for this hunt was well worth it. The men back home in Belle Creek, Montana wouldn't believe this, let alone the women.

I thought of all the problems I had finding hunting clothes to fit me. The many days we waited for all of our ordered gear to arrive. Every time the UPS truck would stop it was like Christmas for Mike and me.

I thought of the 30 pounds I lost while getting my 33-year-old body in shape. The daily four-mile walks and exercise classes. Leaving our two children back home for three weeks. Looking for a pair of hip boots to fit me. The looks I got from people when I told them I was going hunting in Alaska. The long distance phone calls to Ed. The many hours we spent down at the rifle range shooting targets. The rubber boots we cut off for camp boots that we ended up hunting in. The cortisone shot I had to get in my right knee, hopefully preventing it from bothering me during the hunt. Having to go on birth control pills to control my menstrual cycle because we would be in bear country. No make-up or hair washing for days. I felt like I had died and gone to heaven after having all of the planning, preparations and the hunt pass before my smiling eyes.

We decided to field dress the bull after a few pictures were taken. I discovered that my 150-grain Nosler bullet had hit the bull high behind the left front shoulder breaking his spine. We hoped that the small can of black pepper that we sprinkled on the caribou's exposed areas would be enough to discourage the persistent blow flies until morning.

It was getting late, so we had to go down the mountain and cut a trail through the alders so we could backpack out the meat early the next morning. We still had to climb the mountain to our camp, too. I knew the sight of camp and crawling into my sleeping bag on the hard frost-covered ground would feel like checking into a Holiday Inn that night. But now I was anxious to see how Mike had done too. And I couldn't wait to show him my bull.

Mike met us at the bottom of the mountain in the alder patch. We told him about my double-shoveled caribou. He smiled ear to

Carol Rollings' trophy was one of three double-shovel caribou taken on her hunt. Carol said they had a tough time sleeping the last night in camp because they were all grinning so hard.

ear and said, "You aren't going to believe this, but I have a double-shovel down, too!" Three double shovels in one hunt!

The three of us could hardly shut our eyes that night becausewe were smiling so hard. As I laid there trying to go to sleep, visions of trophy bulls and their majestic racks danced before my eyes. It was going to be hard to leave the beauty of this breath-taking state of Alaska. Ed had been a superb outfitter, guide and companion hunter. He never promised us a trophy, or even a shot—just a good time—and that we had!

If someone would have told me a year before my hunt that I would get a caribou that would make the record books, I would have told them they were dreaming. But I guess that's what it is all about—dreaming. Only this dream hunt came true!

8

President's
Trophy Winner

Kentucky Windage
Drops Dall Ram

by Jack Cook

On August 11, 1985, Stan Stevens of MacKenzie Mountain Outfitters called me. After the usual hunting small talk he said, "Jack, I have a cancellation on a sheep hunt; do you know anybody that would be interested? It runs from August 17th to the 31st. I tell you Jack, I'll offer this for half price or better just to fill my guides."

By that time my pulse rate had increased considerably. "Stan," I said, "let me think on it. I may consider taking it myself."

I already had six weeks of conditioning under my belt in preparation for my Alaskan brown bear hunt scheduled for October. This was a vital plus since I know from experience how grueling backpack sheep hunts can be. Also, most of my farm work was done for the time; it had been a dry summer, and what little hay that grew was already safely stored away in the silos. My wife's objections faded after I assured her that she could have a new patio door installed. So I called Stan back later in the day, and told him that I had found him a hunter—if I could hunt with Danny Moore as my guide, and that I couldn't leave until the 18th, since my daughter was getting married on the 17th. Stan readily agreed to meet me at the Norman Wells airport on the 19th.

I love sheep hunting. This was to be my fifth sheep hunt—the second for Dall sheep with Stan and Danny. My first hunt with

Stan had been in 1981, and I had bagged a 38-inch ram and a dandy Mountain Caribou that scored 387⅜ B&C points.

That first day in Norman Wells, Northwest Territories, I stayed at the spacious, rustic log house that Stan had built himself from logs cut in British Columbia and floated up the MacKenzie River. We discussed our hunting plans, and picked up my license and tags at the fish and game offices.

The second day, Stan flew Danny, me, and two pack dogs to one of his famous so-called landing sites! About 150 miles west of Norman Wells, it's a high saddle on top of the mountains. From the air, it looks like a helicopter landing pad, but Stan is a good pilot. "I'll land you fellows here and pick you up on Mountain River in nine or 10 days. Find me a place to land, Danny."

The river is approximately 35 to 40 miles away. After Stan had left us, I asked Dan why Stan was so vague about his pick-up day. Danny explained that he wasn't being vague. He meant that he would pick us up on day nine if weather permitted; otherwise it would be the next day.

From the drop point, this was strictly a backpack hunt. We lived in a two-man tent, ate freeze-dried food and carried everything we needed which amounted to about 50 pounds for each of us and 30-40 pounds for each dog (the dogs had their own packs).

On the second day, we spotted five rams on the mountainside about 15-20 miles north of us. Luckily, it was in the same direction as the river. We couldn't be sure of their size, but Danny thought that at least one was worth a second look at closer range. For two days we picked our way across the rocky terrain. Periodic rain and snow made the footing even more slippery and treacherous. We reached the foot of the mountain where we had seen the rams by late afternoon of the fourth day.

Just before making camp that afternoon, I slipped and fell backwards. My pack broke my fall, but I hit my rifle scope. It was dented around the objective lens bell, but seemed okay otherwise.

We made a dry, quiet, smokeless camp that night since the sheep were only about a five or six hour stalk away. The next morning we rose with the sun. I mentioned to Danny that I hoped I hadn't hurt my scope, but we didn't dare fire my gun since we were so close to the sheep. I was concerned!

We climbed the mountain, but when we got to the top the sheep were nowhere to be seen. We started to glass the heights. Finally, about 150 yards below us across a sharp ravine, we

Life Member Jack Cook, right, had to do some fast calculating to drop this sheep at 300 yards. A fall earlier in the hunt had jarred his scope off target by more than two feet!

spotted one ram lying down. Assuming he was one of the five we had seen earlier, and hoping the big one was close, we dropped to our bellies and started to crawl down the slope. The rams were laying stairstepped down the mountain, so as I made my way down, they came into view one at a time. But the instant I saw each one, they would also see me and jump to their feet. The fifth ram was a beauty, possibly 40-inches plus.

I hastily loaded a round, as the rams started moving slowly away. I touched off a round from my .300 Weatherby Magnum (loaded with a 180-grain Nosler and 82 grains of 4831, my favorite load) and missed big; at least two feet high. What!?! I slammed another round in, held the same place and hit the same place—two feet high. The sheep were moving out fast by then. The third round held under the stomach still hit high grazing the ram's eye lid. The sheep were now about 300 yards or more. The big ram stopped. My mind was frantically trying to calculate some Kentucky windage, knowing that my scope was off. The fourth and killing shot, aimed 12 inches below his belly and 12 inches to the left, broke his back. My years of hunting experience, target shooting and reloading paid big dividends that day.

It was dark by the time we made it back to camp with the meat, horns and full cape. It had been a long, hard day, but very rewarding. We weren't too tired to measure my ram. He taped 40 inches on both sides, and green scored 165. He later scored 163⅜.

The next morning we fixed sheep liver for breakfast, fried in the cast iron pan that we had made the dogs carry and some of the Wisconsin butter I had packed the whole trip just for that reason.

We spent the next two days eating sheep, telling stories and discussing how to mount my trophy. We decided I should mount my sheep life-size since 40-inch rams are such rare trophies.

I did check my rifle during those lazy days. The elevation was off 28 clicks and windage 22 clicks. That fall almost proved fatal to my successful trophy hunt.

Rested and full of sheep meat, (And I do mean full. In 4 days, Danny and I consumed a hind quarter, front quarter, the tenderloins and liver, plus a pound of butter.) we started our long walk down to the river. It took us nearly 13 hours carrying our heavy loads. We spent the next day clearing rocks and driftwood off a gravel bar for Stan to land on. Work done, we got in some fishing while we waited for the clouds to lift. But it was the tenth day of our wilderness adventure before the weather cleared and the Helio Courier single engine World War II reconnaissance plane dropped onto the gravel bar.

Stan flew us to Maclure Lake base camp where we spent the rest of the day visiting with two other successful sheep hunters, a husband and wife team. We caught some lake trout, took long overdue showers and enjoyed some good cooking by Stan's wife, Helen. Then it was back to Norman Wells and home.

Backpack hunting of any kind is an experience never to be forgotten. There are no cars and no radios, just you challenging the elements and the game one-on-one.

9

President's Trophy Winner

My First Grizzly Made The Book

by William Brooks, Sr.

I have álways wanted to go grizzly hunting, but the opportunity never arose until my wife, Mary, and I attended the annual Sportsman Show in Harrisburg, Pennsylvania. It was there we met an outfitter by the name of Bob Hannon.

Mary and I were very impressed with Bob's grizzly hunting success rates, and the longer we talked to him the more I wanted to go bear hunting. After the show, Mary and I talked about the hunt for weeks. I really wanted to go, but couldn't see how we could swing it financially. Mary finally said "You're not getting any younger," called Bob and made reservations.

The next few months were spent shopping for warm clothes and getting in shape. I realized that being in shape would be the most important factor in having a successful hunt.

When the day finally arrived, I flew to Nome, Alaska, to purchase my license and grizzly tag, then to Koyuk, where I spent the next day and a half learning how to walk in snowshoes. Bob showed up late the next day and we flew out in the morning. On the plane, Bob said he had talked to some Eskimos who said they had seen a big bear in our hunting area.

The following day my guide, Barry, and I began hunting. There was over three feet of snow on the ground and I kept tripping on what I thought were twigs but turned out to be the tops of small pine trees. When you fall in such deep snow the natural tendency is to put your hand out to break your fall. Trouble is, your hand breaks right through and you bury your face in the snow. After a day and a half of this, I kept asking myself if I really wanted a bear that bad. The answer was always yes.

We finally found the bear's trail, and started playing catch up. We went up one ridge and down another, putting on mile after mile. My legs were really starting to ache, when I spotted the bear walking up a ridge. The bear must have smelled or heard us because all of a sudden he turned around. I knew he wouldn't stand there for long so I immediately slid a round into the chamber of my .308 Norma Magnum, aimed and fired.

The grizzly didn't even flinch! He just turned and walked up the ridge like nothing had happened. I didn't have time to shoot again.

I began to doubt that I had hit him, but my hold was steady and all the shooting practice I had put in over the summer told me I did.

Barry and I started up the ridge after the bear. When we reached the top we stopped to glass the pines below us to see if the bear was anywhere in sight. When 30 minutes of waiting and glassing failed to turn up anything, we decided to go after him.

While following the bear's tracks down the ridge, Barry told me not to look for the whole bear because he had probably already made his "chute." Barry said a wounded grizzly will walk back and forth to pack down the snow to make it easier for him to attack. I was really glad he told me that at the time.

The tracks lead us through some dense pines and alders. Visibility was very poor. I constantly searched for the bear, watching for movement or his blonde coat.

Suddenly, a humped back and two beady eyes appeared over a snow mound only 20 yards away. The bear was going to charge! I quickly shouldered my gun, put the scope a few inches under his chin so I wouldn't ruin his skull, and fired. The bear dropped when the magnum roared. There was no growling, thrashing or charge. He just dropped dead.

When Barry reached me all he could say was "I thought you would never shoot." Barry, who was behind and above me, had spotted the bear before I had and had watched everything.

After taking a bunch of photos, we skinned the bear. We found out my first shot had entered the chest and exited the arm pit area without hitting any vitals. It was then I realized that I had just walked up to a healthy grizzly.

That night, while lying in the tent, I went over the day's

Bill Brooks' Alaskan grizzly scored 26³/₁₆ and earned him the 1986 NAHC President's Trophy.

events. I couldn't get out of my mind how close I had gotten to the grizzly, and just thinking about what could have happened made my body start to shake. Needless to say I didn't sleep at all that night.

Later, back home in Pennsylvania, I had my bear scored for the Boone and Crockett record book. I was happy to learn that he scored 26³/₁₆, enough to make the record book with room to spare.

10

The Oldest Whitetail In The Woods

by H. John Rice

I was already awake when the alarm sounded at 3:30 a.m. It was November 10th, the first day of Kentucky's split whitetail hunting season. The second season was to follow in December.

David, my 19-year-old son was up too, and we hurriedly dressed while the coffee was brewing. After a quick breakfast, we loaded the pickup with our guns and equipment and headed for the hunting area we had selected, approximately 18 miles away.

If our 14-pointer was to be where we were almost certain he would be at daybreak, we had to keep the wind from him to us. So we zippered up our jackets, shouldered our rifles and headed out on foot to one of three possible positions.

We walked softly through an open field by way of another farm, and circled back to the timber's edge, arriving 45 minutes before the break of dawn, as planned.

We decided after arriving at our stand under a large red cedar tree, to stay together instead of separating. The wind was shifting, and we figured it was better to stay put instead of spreading our scent all over the place. It later proved to be a very wise decision.

This was the third year David and I, as well as many other hunters, had been after this deer. Two years before we had given up, and I shot a small eight-point buck some 500 yards from where we were now standing. When we had finished field dressing it and turned to get some poles to carry him with, we spotted our 14-point buck staring at us 150 yards away. We made the mistake of moving too quickly for our guns, which were leaning against some nearby trees. He was gone in a flash, disappearing over a ridge.

While scouting during the fall, I had watched this 14-point buck go into the large depressed area we were watching and bed down early after feeding on the soybeans. He did, however, bed down a few times in the large timber or broomsedge near where we were standing. We felt certain however on this cold damp day he would go to the large depressed area.

Dawn arrived and it was light enough that we could see the sloping terrain in the valley below. We could not see a deer feeding in the soybean field or even so much as hear one, so we waited. At 6:30 a.m., someone fired from the small patch of large timber below to the right. He fired again; then a third time. Four hundred yards away, over a fence to the west, leaped a big 10-point buck and three does that we knew had run with the 14-pointer at times. David whispered that guy had blown it for us. I whispered, "No, that is not the 14-pointer. Watch the large depressed area."

Almost instantly, David said, "I see movement in the depressed area!" Then I saw it. Behind the first action was a second movement. We spotted a doe coming toward us, a buck was behind her.

"I can't tell how big he is," David whispered. "He's hunched behind the doe, but he's coming this way." I also could not tell what size buck he was.

The doe and buck came toward us. The doe was still in the lead as they passed a large poplar tree in the middle of the field. They stopped on the edge of the soybean acreage.

The buck was behind the poplar slowly raising his head to look over the large limbs. We stood motionless.

His white throat was distinctly visible as he stood still. His silhouette was vaguely visible to us. He managed to obscure his antlers behind the tree and other growth.

The doe, looking back, finally decided to take the center trail to the heavy timber in which we were standing. We felt certain the buck would follow. The buck hesitated, then followed her.

When he came out from behind the tree, I spotted his rack. It was so wide and heavy that it had to be the 14-pointer. I whispered softly to David, and to myself, "Keep it cool. Keep it cool."

I began leading the buck with my Ruger M77 chambered in .280 Remington. When the crosshairs of my Bushnell scope seemed right, I sent the 125-grain Core-Lokt on its way.

NAHC member John Rice, left, and his son David, pose with the mounted head of John's trophy buck. The notch in the right ear of John's buck is believed to have been caused by an ear tag that ripped out. The tag was put on the deer when it was released 15 years earlier.

The buck just stopped and looked back. The doe broke into a run. David quickly centered him in his sights and fired just as the buck took off. He was really moving when I found him in the scope again. I fired when the crosshairs passed his right shoulder. He dropped as the echo of my shot died away. We could see his antlers above the broomsedge 205 yards away.

David and I ran to him. His antlers were non-typical but his rack was beautiful. He had 16 points over an inch long instead of 14. I was so nervous I just could not tag him right then. I just sat down. It had been a long time since I had a seizure of buck fever like this.

We later discovered that David had hit the buck through the outer edge of the liver.

We checked him in at the official check station after we had field dressed him. Without his heart and liver he weighed 214 pounds. His rack was the attraction of the day. The local television station even put him on the sports show several times.

The taxidermist who mounted him told me that when he had finished mounting him and placed him on the wall of his antique shop, 26 people were lined up outside before opening time the next morning to view him.

The deer's inside right ear has a notch in it. It is believed that this is the buck that was trapped with five does at Mammoth Cave National Park and released on the very farm on which we were hunting. The notch is believed to be the result of the lost ear tag.

David's boss told my son that he was the one who hauled the buck and five does to this farm and released them for the local sportsman's club 15 years ago.

A nearby neighbor told me that he had seen this buck for the past 11 years. This is almost unbelievable, as this buck's meat was as tender and succulent as any whitetail I have ever eaten.

Even though I fired the fatal shot, David's assistance made this the most memorable hunt I have ever been on.

11

Two B&C Caribou In One Day

by Glenn Smith

The date was September 17, 1986. I was on top of a treeless hill overlooking the Pons River in northeastern Quebec. The smell of the tundra and the clean cool air almost made me forget why I was there. It turned out to be a day I'll never forget.

My partners included my father Richard Smith, from Medina, Ohio; NAHC member Don Smith, from North Royalton, Ohio; Bob Smock, from Meadville, Pennsylvania; and NAHC member Ken Hudson from Brunswick, Ohio. We were hunting Quebec-Labrador caribou with Jack Hume, owner of Laurentian Ungava Outfitters. We chose Jack after checking on several outfitters. He has a very good reputation and came highly recommended.

Our trip from Medina, Ohio, to Shefferville, Quebec, got off to a bad start. On our way to catch a commercial flight in Montreal, one of the pickups lost its transmission. After getting switched to another vehicle; we finally made it to the Montreal airport only to find that our flight to Shefferville was canceled because of weather. We eventually took off and made it to Shefferville, but found the weather had grounded all the bush planes in the area for several days. One and a half days later, we were flown to one of Jack's outpost camps about 135 miles northwest of Shefferville.

Unless you have flown over the tundra, it is hard to imagine the desolation of northern Quebec. All you see is mile after mile of bog interspersed with rivers, lakes, and small rocky mountains

Glenn Smith with the first of two Boone & Crockett Quebec-Labrador caribou bulls he took in a single day.

covered with caribou moss and stunted pines. About half way out, we started spotting caribou on the ground, making us even more anxious to get started.

After getting to camp, we met our guide, NAHC member Raymond Desjardines. Raymond told us to wait and look over a few bulls before taking any. Any mature bull will look mighty impressive. He said the five hunters of the previous week, shot eight bulls their first afternoon and got the last two the next morning. The rest of the week they saw many larger bulls and wished they had not been so hasty in filling their tags.

After getting our gear organized, we all went out for the rest of the afternoon. None of us could believe what we were seeing. There were caribou everywhere. I saw over 300 animals, about half of them bulls. I made up my mind not to shoot that first day. I just watched and took pictures. Bob was the only one to take an animal that afternoon

The next morning, Raymond took everyone out to the areas they would hunt by canoe. I stayed with him and we walked up into the surrounding hills. There were so many caribou, it's a wonder we did not get trampled. We had a herd of 22 come right at us and pass on both sides of the rock we were behind. Raymond had to hold me down to keep from shooting. He reminded me that there were bigger bulls around, but I found that hard to believe. While we were watching, he explained what to look for in a good rack. I spent the rest of the day studying and comparing antlers and took a number of magnificent photographs. That day, my dad took two big bulls, and Don took one that green scored well above the Boone and Crockett minimum of 375 points. Bob took a huge double shovel that later scored 399⅜ Boone and Crockett points.

The next day, after one of Ken's super breakfasts, I walked to the top of the hill above a caribou crossing on the Pons River. A few caribou crossed the river during the first couple hours I was there, but none were real big. I had my spotting scope set up on a rock so I could look them over closely as they swam across the river. About 10:00 a.m., a herd of 14 bulls jumped in and started towards me. I could see immediately there was a good bull in the bunch. He had huge palmated antlers with long points. The bottom looked good too, so I decided to take him. He was still in full velvet, which made him look even more impressive. I moved down the ridge, to where the trail came up through the scrub pines. My Winchester Model 70 in .300 Winchester Magnum did its job well. When I walked up to him, only then did I realize what a magnificent animal he really was. While I was dressing him, several groups of caribou passed within 50 feet of me. I took lots of good pictures.

I went back up on top and continued watching for the rest of the day. About 4:00 in the afternoon, I saw a lone bull start across. I could see that he had good double shovels and decided that he was good enough for my second animal.

When Raymond came with the canoe to pick me up, he got very excited. He told me that both heads would probably make the book. We loaded everything into the canoe and started down stream to camp. We had a big load and some bad rapids to go through. Rather than risk getting dumped in the icy water, we put ashore and led the canoe through the rapids with a long rope. With all the bog and high brush along the bank, we managed to get about as wet as if we had tried to run the rapids and capsized.

Back at camp, we green scored my heads and the one with the big palmated antlers scored just over 400 and the double shovel scored just over 380 points.

At that point, the five of us had taken 10 caribou four of which were record size. Raymond still had his tags, so we invited him to hunt. My dad said he would guide for him. Dad did a pretty

Glenn Smith and his two record book racks taken the same day on a hunt with Laurentian Ungava Outfitters out of Schefferville, Quebec, Canada.

good job as Raymond took two good bulls including a nice double shovel. These two bulls were also well above the minimum of 375 to qualify for the record book. For the week, we took 12 bulls, six of them Boone and Crockett qualifiers.

After the required 60-day drying period, my two caribou, when officially measured, scored 375 even and 396⅜. Two record book caribou on the same day. I'll never forget September 17, 1986.

12

President's
Trophy Winner

Nine Years
To A Record Grizzly

by Harry Leggett, Jr.

The quest for a trophy grizzly bear started in 1968 with my first hunt in Canada. Although I was in excellent grizzly country and had a successful hunt for moose and caribou, I never even saw a grizzly. The guides did tell numerous stories about the grizzly, not the typical stories about a snarling, ferocious monster, but about his wariness, sense of smell, cunning and intelligence. I was fascinated.

I returned to British Columbia in 1969 and had a successful hunt for goat and caribou. It was on this trip that I saw my first grizzly. The die was cast; I wanted a big bear.

In 1972, I teamed up with my hunting buddy, Kniebert Stillman of Peach Orchard, Missouri. We both had a goal: To put a brown or grizzly in the record book. We read, talked to hunters and guides and decided three things: 1) A combination hunt might be great but it wasn't the best way to get a record book bear; we had to concentrate on one animal. 2) We had to be in the right area—Kodiak Island for browns or the coast of British Columbia for grizzlies. 3) We had to have patience.

Eight years later, on September 30, 1980, we left Little Rock, Arkansas, on our ninth hunt. Nine hunts exclusively for bear—120 hunting days, countless dollars spent, endless miles traveled. We had been cold, wet, hot, dry, wind-blown, sun-burned and fog-bound. During that time, we had seen at least 100 bear, stalked about 20 and passed up around 10 good, adult animals. We had strained our marriages and, at times, our friendship. We experienced boredom, excitement, frustration and anger. We were being terrorized by the singleness of our purpose—we wanted one in the book.

We left Little Rock and flew to Campbell River, British Columbia to meet our guide and good friend, Jack Innes. On the morning of September 30th, we boarded his boat, the *Estero*, and proceeded to our hunting grounds about 100 miles up the coast. The first stop was a quiet, remote area where we had seen a huge, black-coated grizzly the year before.

On October 1st, we spent the morning scouting the area for bear signs. There were a lot of dog salmon in the river and fresh sign of at least two large grizzlies, but things didn't look all that great. It was time to look over the Wakeman River area located about 25 miles away.

The first hints of trouble started about 10 miles from our destination. The usually clear ocean waters took on a muddy, almost brown color which could only mean the Wakeman was flooding. Our confidence fell to near zero when these fears were confirmed. The Wakeman had flooded, pushing most of the spawning fish back to the ocean, making the bear hunting very difficult. We had seen several grizzlies in this area during previous hunts, a couple of which were record size, so we decided to take a look around anyway. We docked and talked to our friends at a logging camp. They informed us that, while the Wakeman had indeed flooded, another river, the Atway, about six miles up the valley, had not. We decided to start the next morning at the junction of the Wakeman and the Atway.

We left the boat the next morning before daylight. It was a beautiful fall morning, but the Wakeman was so muddy, our confidence level, on a scale of one to 10, was a zero.

About 200 yards below the Atway River we saw the tracks of a very large bear—and they were obviously fresh. Now, one set of bear tracks does not make a bear hunt, but a hunter's confidence and adrenaline operate somewhat like a yo-yo. Our confidence jumped from zero to 10.

After a brief discussion, we decided that Kniebert would stay to watch the riffle at the junction of the rivers and Jack and I would circle upstream, cross the Atway and check out the shoals above the junction of the rivers. While this was about a half-mile circle, it only placed us about 300 yards apart. Separated by heavy brush,

Harry Leggett, left, and his hunting friend Kniebert Stillman spent nine years in pursuit of this record book grizzly.

our parting words were, "If you hear a shot, it'll be a stud."

Jack and I circled upstream and crossed the Atway. Just as we approached the junction of the rivers, I saw him—my bear! He was walking out of the brush onto a gravel bar at the edge of the river. He was about 50 yards from me, standing broadside and upwind.

One of the things I have learned on my many hunts is how difficult it is to determine the size of a bear. All adult grizzlies look big. I held that bear in my scope while Jack studied it through his binoculars for what seemed like 20 minutes, but it was probably only 20 seconds.

"You better take him," he whispered.

I fired. The bear jumped. I fired again. The bear fell in the river and sank.

All hell broke loose. The river at this point was about five feet deep and swift. Jack had lost a bear in the same section of the river a few years earlier and we didn't want that to happen again.

"Quick! Back to Kniebert!" he screamed as we ran

downstream to where Kniebert was waiting. Jack, being in better physical condition, arrived below the bear before I did. He immediately teamed up with Kniebert and searched the muddy waters of the Wakeman River for the bear. Nothing. They were both sick thinking we had lost him.

Thankfully, I was spared this trauma. They spotted the dead bear just as I reached them. It was hung up in a snag about 50 feet from the bank. Kniebert and I charged out, grabbed a foot and dislodged the bear from the snag. A thousand pounds of bear in three and a half feet of freezing, roaring water put us to the test, but we had him, and a winch couldn't have pulled him away from us.

Jack scrambled to his pack for a rope and threw it to us. We tied it to a leg, held on, and let the current work the bear into the bank. Then we realized what a monster we had. His weight? We will never know, but the three of us were unable to roll him over. The skull measured 26 $^{11}/_{16}$ and the hide squared 9-feet, 10-inches.

We had done it! Not only did we have a record class grizzly, but perhaps one as big or bigger than any other ever collected in fair chase.

Now, my story might be more entertaining if I could tell of superb marksmanship and a three-day stalk, or if this bear had been a charging, snarling, slobbering beast killed in full charge at only four yards. But neither would be the truth.

We persevered and got our trophy—I say "we" because the sighting down the rifle and the pulling of the trigger represented only about 20 seconds out of nine years in *our* quest for this animal.

13

Whitetail: The Ultimate Challenge

by Dick Scorzafava

During late August, I had been reconnoitering my favorite hunting area in the western end of my home state, Massachusetts, when I spotted a huge buck in velvet at the edge of a meadow. I have taken many bucks over the years, but had never seen a Massachusetts buck with such an exceptional rack as this one. I decided at that moment that this buck would be my quarry for the 1985 archery season. Win or lose, I would not take a shot at another animal.

I did my homework. I studied the buck's area well and had gained even more knowledge from topographical maps. I acquired a good knowledge of the principles of wind thermals. I had done my pre-season scouting, watching the whitetail buck, watching for signs, learning his habits and determining which scrapes were boundary, secondary and primary. For a whitetail to be considered a big buck he must have lived approximately 5½-7½ years and have been fortunate to have the benefit of good genetics, good feed and moderate wintering. Knowing this made my quest even more important, as I knew the buck was the outstanding individual in his area.

I practice with my bow an average of twice a week during the off season, but usually increase my practice in August when I try to shoot every day in natural settings from all different angles and positions varying my distance from five out to 35 yards. My bow is a Black Widow recurve, 68 pounds at 29½ inches. I do not use a sight, a release or an arrow rest. I shoot instinctively, off the shelf of the bow. I have a Black Widow quiver mounted on the bow and it holds my XX75 Easton shafts with turkey feathers and Snuffer broadheads.

Opening day finally arrived. I was eager and excited and felt confident that all of my pre-season work would do me well, but I knew that I still was matching wits with a survivor on his home turf. I would need to be able to use all of my acquired hunting knowledge and skills to try and overcome the edge that nature had given him.

I had the approach to the morning stand preplanned, to keep the wind thermals in my favor and to try and keep the deer population from scenting me. I reached my stand and realized that the hardest part of my hunt was about to begin...the waiting. One must not make any noise, and strictly limit movement of any kind. Patience is not one of my outstanding virtues and I really have to make an effort to remain in a tree all day.

By late morning, all I had seen was a small six-point buck and a few does. The next few days were just as uneventful as deer movement slowed. I passed up a shot at a subordinate 8-point buck during the second week of the season as he came to the scrape I was watching. Then I saw him. My adrenalin began flowing, my heart pounded and hammered in my ears. Here I was looking at a magnificent specimen of the whitetail deer, a record book entry if I had ever seen one. My anticipation mounted...unfortunately he never got close enough for me to take a shot. That evening, as I returned home, I was very disappointed and frustrated.

The third week of the season began, and it was the last day that I would be able to hunt. I took up the vigil at my morning stand, and as morning dawned the 10-pointer returned. The minutes crawled by as he picked his way through the cover. He kept his nose into the wind straining to pick up the slightest scent of danger. I held my breath. I hoped he couldn't hear the deafening beat of my heart. Finally, he reached the primary scrape and proceeded to hoof up the area. He freshened the scrape and next he raised his head, with a magnificent 10-point rack that I was sure would find a place in the record books, into the branches of a nearby tree and began rubbing.

This ritual gave me the cover I needed to draw my Black Widow recurve. I drew the XX75 shaft and focused on a spot high in his lung area. I was shooting from a high angle and I hoped my

Like Dick Scorzafava many NAHC members consider a trophy whitetail the ultimate hunting challenge.

Massachusetts isn't often thought of as the home of monster whitetails, but Dick Scorzafava's bow-killed buck crushes that myth.

arrow would pass through both lungs. I wanted to achieve a good spill-over as it ruptured the second lung. I released and the Snuffer-tipped arrow found its mark...a perfect hit. The buck lowered his head, shook his body and walked away. He didn't go far. Less than 25 yards later he stopped and fell to the ground. It was over.

As I descended my perch and approached the buck, I felt a sense of satisfaction and accomplishment. I had accepted the challenge and one-on-one we had played the scene out till its very end. I felt that I had mastered the ultimate challenge. I had had a successful hunt, but not just any hunt, it was the hunt of a lifetime. The crowning jewel was the buck's Pope & Young score of 162⅛ points.

14

Great Friends Led
Me To A Trophy Bull

by Santo Marzocca

E arly in 1985, I applied for special area antelope and elk permits in my home state of Wyoming. The elk permit I applied for was in Grand Teton National Park, which was limited to 1,000 permits that year. Previous years had limits as high as 2,500-3,000 permits, but due to some unforseen events, it was reduced to 1,000. As lady luck would have it, I drew one of these permits. I also drew an antelope permit. That's the good news.

The bad news is I reinjured my lower back in late June while pulling the engine out of a truck. I'm an auto and truck mechanic and live in Cody. I had originally injured my back in February of 1984.

I missed out on my antelope hunt because I could not walk without excruciating pain. My doctor put me in a physical therapy program which helped, but I still could not walk very far without feeling some discomfort. I decided that it was a good idea to cancel my elk hunt as well. I informed the rest of my hunting party that I would be unable to hunt with them. In the meantime, I had been successful in a drawing for a special hunting area inside the park, a small mountain called Blacktail Butte. When my friends heard that I wouldn't be going with them, they held a meeting to discuss my dilemma. They called me and asked if I would come to Casper to discuss the situation. When we met, my friends had already decided that I was going on the hunt, even if they would have to carry me. I thought it was a tremendous gesture on their part, and I almost cried. I thought to myself, "These are what you call real friends." We made our plans.

My closest friend, Jack Barrows, whom is like a brother to me, said he would pick me up, hook up my camper trailer and take us to the park to meet the rest of our hunting party. We made camp just outside the park at the KOA campground, a day before the season opened. The season in the special area began October 25 and ended November 1 that year.

For the next several mornings, my friends would drive me to my hunting area and leave me in a position with a pretty good view of the area. They would pick me up again at lunch and take me back to camp so I could lay down and rest. The rest of the party would then hunt the rest of the day.

I saw elk almost every day, but they were too far to take a good killing shot. I teach hunter safety and education here in Cody for the Wyoming Fish & Game Department and frown on any shot that is not going to be fatal.

The day I got my bull started out fast. Early in the morning, I spotted a herd of elk about 1,500 yards away. As I was watching them, some other hunters fired at them and they started moving toward my position. I was sitting in a gully which was about seven feet deep and 10 feet wide. I would have to follow it about 500 yards if I wanted to get within range of them.

It was difficult going. I had to sit or lie down every few yards to rest. Occasionally, I would look up out of the gully to see where

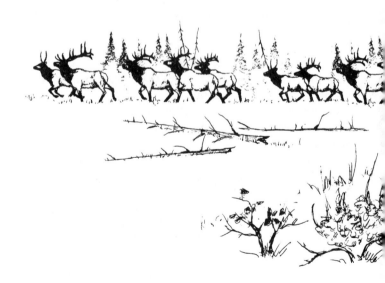

the elk were headed, then duck back down and continue on. After what seemed like ages, I finally reached the end of the gully. I crawled up to the trees and to my surprise, the elk were coming right toward me—and they were only 50 yards away! I counted 35 bulls and one cow in the herd. I quickly looked up and down the line of animals trying to pick out the biggest bull as they trotted past me in a single line. The decision was easy as one of the most magnificent bulls I had ever seen in the wild came into view. I quickly found him in my scope, aimed carefully and pulled the trigger. The bull dropped as if he had been hit with a sledge hammer. He was a fine 6x6 and almost as big as a horse.

My friend Jack Barrows, shot a nice 5x5 as it passed about 75 yards to my right and 225 yards from Jack.

I was using a .300 Weatherby Magnum with my handloads, which were 180-grain Nosler Partition bullets with Weatherby brass. I have used this rifle for all my game, from prairie dogs to elk and bear. I know my rifle very well and know what it can do. I just handload up or down to suit the game I am hunting.

Our party got together at the kill site and took some pictures and B.S.'d about the elk we had downed. My friends all congratulated me on the fine trophy I had taken. Now came the

good part for me and the hard part for the rest of the party. It sure was nice to lie back on the grass and watch, while they cleaned and skinned my elk for me. This all started at about 9:00 a.m. and it took them until 7:30 p.m. to finish most of the work. They still had to go back in the next morning to bring out the front half of my elk.

I do not think I can ever repay my friends for what they did for me in making this one of the most enjoyable and fulfilling hunts I have been on.

15

Caribowhunting

by Carl G. Esterly

It was a cold, crisp, cloudy morning. A coat of light frost covered everything in the small town of Schefferville, Quebec. I waited and watched as members of Laurentian Ungava Outfitters loaded the float plane with my equipment and five days worth of supplies. I was about to start a bowhunt for Quebec-Labrador caribou in Quebec's subarctic tundra called "Ungava."

In this part of the country, you live with your binoculars if you want any chance of seeing caribou. The land is barren except for a few trees which grow only to a height of about six feet, making visibility excellent.

It was sleeting, raining and blowing with a temperature of about 29 degrees when we started hunting the next day, but the temperature was overlooked as numerous caribou were spotted. We saw a total of 27 caribou that day, seven of which were decent-looking bulls. John, my guide, said these were "scrappers," meaning they weren't any good. They all looked like fine bulls to me especially after hunting whitetail deer in Pennsylvania for so many years.

The weather cleared the next day and warmed up to 60 degrees, making hunting difficult for the next few days. We hunted hard the entire time, walking constantly and glassing from various vantage points. We saw only three cow caribou the second day, and even fewer the next two.

As I laid in the tent the night before the last day of my hunt, all kinds of things started going through my mind. Earlier that night, my two rifle-hunting companions, who had already taken their bulls, were getting on my case about why I didn't try and take one of the bulls I had seen the first day. I was praying the weather would change, not knowing if it would as there was no communication with the outside world. My prayers were answered! I woke up about 4:30 to find the wind blowing and sleet coming down.

When daylight came, John and I were off. Visibility was down to just a couple of hundred yards. We reached the top of the ridge where we started hunting on the first day, and found a herd of 17 caribou. Five were young bulls and three were fair size. We had put on an hour-and-a-half stalk. John asked me if I wanted to try and take one of the bulls, but I said, "No, John, it's still early." I felt good because the weather was totally rotten and the bulls were moving.

We moved back up to the ridge. By this time the snow had ceased, but there was a fine mist coming down. Visibility grew when the snow stopped. We saw six more caribou about three quarters of a mile across the terrain and started the stalk for a closer look. When we got within 100 yards, we saw that there were two decent-sized bulls, but I could not get within the range I needed for a good bow shot.

John told me, "Don't worry, Carl. We saw more bulls this morning than we saw in the last three days. Don't get excited. We'll get a bigger one than your friends got and show them."

John said we should wait there 15 or 20 minutes and if we didn't see anything, we'd move down the lake. So, we waited and watched. Then we hiked to the other end of the lake. We came across one fine-looking bull, but we couldn't get within 300 yards of him. As we approached the other end of the lake, we started staring through our binoculars, looking at every inch of the terrain; sitting there waiting and looking. John suddenly hollered, "Bulls! Let's go!" As we ran down the valley he told me that they were just over the other ridge.

We stayed low until we got to the ridge. I was beat by the time we got there. John was definitely excited. We crawled over the top of the ridge on our bellies and peeked over. Almost immediately I spotted three huge bulls, but they were over 1,000 yards away. And there was no cover for us to make a stalk. Our only option was to back down the slope and try to get in front of the bulls.

Carl Esterly made a 60-yard running shot to tag this 358-point Pope & Young Quebec Labrador caribou.

The excitement hit when we started easing into range. My legs started to shake and I could hardly walk. John kept telling me to stay low or they would spot us. The ridge was U-shaped, so we went right up the middle.

We were very cautious when we reached the top. John looked around and said, ''They're gone.'' I looked. My heart sank. There was no time for another stalk, my chance for a fine bull was gone.

I stood up with a sinking feeling, looked to my left and spotted the bulls about 55 to 60 yards away watching us.

John whispered, ''Take the leader, he's the biggest.'' I drew my 68-pound Jennings Arrowstar compound, and when I did, the bulls took off. I thought to myself, ''It's now or never.''

I lead the first bull by about 10 feet and released the Wasp-tipped 2016 Easton XX75 arrow. The arrow looked like it was in slow motion as I watched it in flight.

The arrow ripped high into the bull's shoulder, making a loud ''crack'' as it hit bone. John hollered, ''Great shot!'' and looked at me with amazement in his eyes. I was just as surprised.

We watched as the caribou ran down the hill, not knowing which one was hit because they kept switching places. We waited 20 minutes before we started to follow them. A little while later, we came across all three caribou laying down. We snuck on our bellies within 40 yards of them.

Two of them jumped up and started to run. They looked beautiful. The one that was hit also started to get up, slowly coming to a full stance. I drew my bow and released again, making a direct heart shot. The caribou ran about 50 yards before taking a nose-dive. He was dead.

John and I jumped up and down with joy as we ran to my caribou. John told me we had taken a fine bull, in fact, the largest one in camp all year. He later scored 358 Pope & Young points.

Many times as I stood in my yard practicing with my bow, I dreamed about going somewhere and shooting a record book animal. Well, my dream came true.

16

A "Look-See" Blacktail

by Bill Bechens

"He is magnificent," I thought to myself as I stared at the fat, healthy blacktail buck laying at my feet. My 10 years of bowhunting flashed through my mind. I'd been privileged to have been on many fine hunts and to have taken a number of other animals, but all the previous animals had been essentially luck. Somehow, this hunt had been different; the sighting, the multiple stalks, the other animals I had to avoid, the wind and finally the shot itself. Everything flowed together so smoothly. "And to think I didn't even plan to hunt today!"

Wednesday, the 21st of November, 1984, began like any other work day; up at 6:30 a.m., a quick cup of black coffee and off for the hospital to make morning rounds before the office routine began. I'd been on call the previous weekend and couldn't go hunting; it stormed Monday and Tuesday, but I wasn't able to get done early enough those evenings to hunt either. The Oregon archery deer season would soon close, and I still was the proud possessor of a valid tag. Oh well, it was no matter; I had four days off coming up over the Thanksgiving weekend.

It had been an unusual year. Bill Jr. and I had actually found some preseason time to scout, and had I been a betting man, I would have wagered both of us a deer and bear in the freezer before the opening weekend closed. We had found a lovely location to hunt deer where there would be only two other hunters, this on some 2,800 acres of prime mule deer range; and the bears had been ripping our baits daily since mid-July. To make a long story short, I had the privilege of being at my son's side when he arrowed a nice 2x2 muley buck on the 8th day of September, and since that time, including a 10-day trip to western Montana, I had not seen a buck. The bears were still ripping the baits to the tune of 50 to 80 gallons of meat per week, but had not allowed themselves to be seen, even for pictures or pleasure.

Winter had begun a good month earlier than usual for our area, and no one was doing real well. The animals just were not doing their usual thing, and even the really top-notch woodsmen and hunters of our area were having difficulty locating game.

By the time I walked out of the hospital with rounds finished and headed for my office, the sun was up, the skies were clear, cold, and a deep azure blue. I really did not want to work, knowing the deer would be up and moving after being holed up by the storm for two days. Fate plays strange tricks and favors sometimes; seems as if many of the patients scheduled for that day had forgotten it was the day before Thanksgiving, and by 10:30, many had canceled to leave town or to do last minute shopping. At any rate, by 11:30, I found myself done for the day and headed home.

Reaching home, I surveyed the day's mail as I changed into my hunting gear, and debated what to fix for lunch, as this was Donna, my very tolerant wife's day to bowl and shop. I made a couple peanut butter and jelly sandwiches, poured a tall glass of cold milk and sat down to eat. As I ate, I wrote my usual note to Donna, something I frequently do during hunting season, as I tend to hunt alone quite often.

"D.B., hope you bowled well today. No word yet from the kids. I've gone to check the bear bait and then will probably look for some deer — SB's or HM. Don't worry, but I'll probably be late tonight — fat chance — Ha! Ha!"

On my way out the door, I grabbed a couple of five gallon cans of bait before I jumped in my truck. It's about 30 miles to the bear bait, and another 25 to reach a legal deer hunting area.

When I reached my bear bait, it was obvious the bear had not been in for the four or five days. "Perhaps he is hibernating by now," I thought as I surveyed the scene. Lots of squirrels, birds and coyotes had been in, but the 50 gallon drum chained to the tree was still quite full and emitting waves of scent that any bear would find hard to resist. I added the 10 gallons of bait that I'd brought and returned to my rig thinking about where best to spend the rest of the afternoon in search of deer.

Both areas were in the same general direction, and as I traveled along the bare highway flanked by the previous two days' snowfall, I decided to try the one I'd not hunted yet. The area was the farthest away, but I felt that maybe the storm would have driven some deer into it. The area itself is along the ridge that tops out at about 4,500 feet, and is timbered across its top and northern slope, with scattered timber and scrub oaks along its steep south face. As I crested the Cascade summit and dropped down the western side, the clear skies turned to ashen gray, full of clouds and fog, with only occasional glimpses of the sun. I finally reached my turn off, and drove up and over the northern side. I was astounded at the amount of snow, and had to drop into four-wheel-drive to get up and over the last half mile or so.

Parking the rig, I carefully checked over my equipment, including the gear I carry in my belt pack, to make sure all was there and functional. I elected not to change from my knee high rubber boots that I wear into the bear bait and on stand. I decided to shoot a couple of blunts out of my 61-pound PSE Laser Magnum to loosen up a bit. Both arrows seemed to fly true into the mark on the snow some 20 yards away, and the bow appeared quite smooth and quiet. Satisfied, I threw the blunts behind the seat, locked the doors and carefully placed the keys in the bottom of a zippered pocket of my camo jacket. I really wasn't very happy with myself, having neglected to throw in my white camo, but decided the green and brown would just have to do; after all, this was just kind of a "look-see" trip to prepare for the long Thanksgiving weekend hunt.

I moved briskly down from the truck along the western edge of the flat until I reached the top border of scrub oaks that bordered its southern side. The snow was soft and basically quiet, but occasionally crunchy. The oak leaves beneath, however, were still dry and noisy. Suddenly, there were lots of deer tracks; no obvious "buck" tracks, but enough other ones to get excited about. I stood in a small patch of oaks for a bit debating whether or not to drop further down the slope, deeper into the oaks, in hopes of finding more open ground. The wind was basically downhill and easterly, but occasionally swirled, especially when the fog moved in tight.

I elected to hunt a sidehill to the east, staying as much as possible within the cover of the oaks lining the bottom of the big flat—constantly reminding myself to move slowly. After perhaps 75 yards, I noted a movement in the oaks below me. I slipped into some nearby foliage, and started glassing the area with my 7x26 Bushnells that I always carry. I eventually spotted two does and three yearlings in the oaks about 80 yards below me. I watched them for a while but nothing else showed. I really had no intentions of taking a doe with young anyway.

I was continuing to slip along the treeline, stopping often to look and listen. It wasn't long before I spotted two more does moving briskly downhill ahead of me. I let them go and continued on my way. I reached a little trickle of a creek that dribbled down from the flat above and spotted yet another doe browsing contentedly below me. There were two more does with her, both in prime shape and dry. I debated trying for one of them, but as I sat planning a route of approach they fed off down the creek bed and out of sight. Lazy, I guess, but I really didn't want to take a doe way down on that snowy steep slick sidehill, and have to pack her up. A buck yes, but not a doe. I'm not a true trophy hunter. I just love to bowhunt, and if possible, eat venison!

I crossed the creek and moved up the hill about 30 yards to a pile of rocks that allowed me to sit with a good view in all directions when the fog wasn't socked in. The slight wind remained rather consistent, always blowing downhill. I lit a cigarette and leaned back against one of the rocks to gaze upward while silently thinking. The kids were coming home from college that afternoon for their Thanksgiving break and I was looking forward to seeing them. I thought about the note I'd left for D.B.; no way I'd be late.

Then suddenly, reality was at hand, as I saw some motion above and to my right. Staring intently, I could make out a pair of deer legs moving slowly from right to left through the foggy mist. Using my binoculars, I found the total outline of the deer as it browsed through some scattered oaks above. It was a buck, a 2x2 with about a 18-inch spread. Now, how to get to him? He was about 100 yards uphill. It appeared that if he continued on his present course, he would angle down and across toward the oaks I'd come through earlier.

Looking back to the left, it appeared that I might be able to cut him off. Using the trunk of one large pine tree as cover, I began to inch my way up to the buck, moving only when his head was down feeding. I'd gone perhaps 25-35 yards before I had to stop. Ahead of me was a 35-foot opening, without enough cover with which to blend. As I knelt there, pondering my next move, a second, and then a third buck materialized from the same direction whence the first had come. One buck was an excellent 4x4 with about a 28-inch spread. The other was a small forked horn.

"Now what?" I thought. "No bucks for 10 weeks and now three of them!" The dilemma was terrible, but the sight was beautiful. As I watched and considered my next move all three browsed slowly up the hill into a small stand of scrub oaks and out of sight. I just sat back, tried to relax, and watched for about five minutes. Nothing happened. I decided to follow them, hoping to get close enough for a shot. They had been in no real hurry, so things looked good.

When I crested the ridge, I cautiously took a look around. About 75 yards out, the first 2x2 was feeding without a care in the world. I sneaked up to a lone pine with low hanging boughs and sat beneath it with my back against the trunk. Using my field glasses, I watched the forkie contentedly browsing while searching intensely for the other two bucks. Unable to locate them after several minutes, I decided to again try for the 2x2, who by then had fed into some oaks with enough cover to sneak within 40-45 yards of him. I eased out from behind the tree and started to inch my way toward the buck. About midway through a draw, I reached another open area, less wide than the first one, but still large enough to concern me. The buck was feeding with his head down and facing away from me, so I figured it would be safe to cross. Five steps later, the 4x4 caught me in mid-stride. I froze, but it was too late. The 2x2 knew something was up and simply walked off. He was joined by the smaller 2x2. The 4x4 didn't leave, he just stared at me for the next 25 minutes trying to figure out what I was. I tried to remain motionless and avoid direct eye contact. Eventually, the buck decided that I was nothing to fear and began walking up the hill, browsing as he went. Boy, did my muscles ache as I released the tension.

I decided to let things cool off a bit. I also hoped to find some better cover by which to again work back up after the three bucks. I was sure that they were not spooked badly and probably would not venture very far. I dropped into the timber to a finger which ran up the slope I had been traversing. I hadn't gone 30 feet before I spotted a doe feeding below me. Closer inspection revealed that she had three yearlings with her. The deer, unfortunately, were between me and the bucks—and heading my way. If they spooked, they would blow any chance I had left to stalk the bucks. I had to think of a way to get them to move, but not scare them into head-long flight.

An idea came to me as I crawled behind a pine tree to watch them. Quietly and slowly I removed an arrow from my quiver, and gingerly stuck the fletched end from behind the tree trunk, moving it ever so slowly. The closest yearling saw it almost immediately and moved over to the doe. She ceased her feeding and stared intently at the fletching, then she slowly advanced toward it. She stopped about 35 yards away, stomped her front feet firmly, and with a gentle, but affirmative sweep of her head, moved into the woods along a sidehill followed by the three yearlings.

With slightly more freedom, I moved up the draw toward the spot I had last seen the bucks. Almost immediately, I spotted another deer browsing along the edge of the timber on the other side of the draw. I thought I caught a glint of sunlight off his antlers, so I decided to investigate further. With a steady breeze and noise from the creek covering my movements, I dropped into the bottom of the draw, crossed the creek, and headed up the other side until I was within 25 feet of the bottom of the flat where I had seen the deer. I took my glasses out again and tried to relocate the buck. Several minutes of searching failed to uncover the buck. Where had he gone now? I was certain that he'd not gotten even with or below me, and decided he'd either gone up deeper into the timber or further east along the edge of the flat. I elected to cross the flat, and slowly edged onto it. That's when I spotted him only 70 yards to my right, standing in full view on a small, open shelf. I was certain he hadn't detected me, so I backed up again. From there, I moved slowly down to an area about 50 yards away that had islands of scrub oak extending all the way up to the base of the bench on which the buck was feeding. I felt my first real twinges of excitement as I surveyed the cover. If he stayed put, I would have a 20-yard shot!

I removed an arrow from my quiver, checked the nock and fletching, twisted the broadhead to be certain that no blades were loose, then slowly started upward, moving only when his head was down or when he was looking away.

Suddenly, the buck looked up and walked out of sight! I almost panicked, figuring my hunt was over, when he reemerged from the brush walking directly at me! I couldn't move without being detected, so I sat as still as possible, watching the buck through squinted eyes. The buck suddenly turned again when he reached the trail of the does I had scared away earlier.

"It's now or never," I said to myself. "He is just going to walk away if I don't shoot." Concentrating on a spot directly

Bill Bechens bagged his trophy blacktail on a day that he hadn't even planned to go deer hunting.

behind his right shoulder and with the bow slightly canted, I drew and released as soon as everything looked "right."

The arrow seemed to be there almost before the release. I noticed the fletching in his side as he raced away, and silently cursed to myself because it appeared to be about four to six inches too far back. I stood from where I'd shot trembling a bit now, lit a cigarette and glanced at my watch. It had been two and a half hours since leaving the truck, and 95 minutes since encountering the first 2x2 buck. The entire hunt had covered less than 800 yards.

I couldn't stand it any longer; a whole five minutes had passed. I threw the cigarette to the snow, stomped it out firmly, and slowly paced the distance to where the buck was when hit—46 yards. I could see where he'd churned the snow and ground as he lunged, but there was no hair or blood immediately visible. I began to follow his tracks, taking two or three steps at a time, and after about ten yards or so, noticed the bright red blood that began to appear on both sides of the track in the snow. At this point I felt somewhat better about the actual arrow placement.

Inching my way down, glassing the entire time, I reached the edge of a small knob. Fifty yards below me, beneath a huge Ponderosa pine, lay the buck. I sat down, glassed his chest, and concluded that he had expired. He was finally mine.

The arrow had done its job, swiftly, painlessly, and efficiently. It went through his liver and left lung—he expired on the run, 102 yards from where he'd been hit.

I took a few pictures after cleaning him up, then field dressed him. He was magnificent with good brow tines and a heavy mahogany colored rack, which later scored 118 P&Y points.

17

My Grizzly Guide Carried a .30-30

by Wes Blakeman

L ooking through his binoculars, my guide said it was a monster of a grizzly; the largest he had ever seen. He whistled to stop the bear. It worked! The big griz immediately stood on his hind legs and stared straight at us. Peering through my rifle scope, it didn't take long to decide that this was the bear I wanted. My guide whispered, "Shoot."

This hunt was the culmination of a lot of planning. Ten months before departure I started checking out references supplied to me by Art Kolp of International Hunting Consultants in Sacramento, California. After many hours on the phone, I booked a mixed bag hunt for myself and three hunting partners Arnold Goodman, John Scianna and my brother Monty, with Mr. Hank Foley of Buckinghorse Ranch, Besa River Outfitters, in northeastern British Columbia. It was a 10-day hunt for moose, wolf, goat, elk and black bear. I was able to get the last grizzly permit, so I was to stay an additional five days hunting for a bear. This was my first long range hunt with these three hunting companions, so all the travel arrangements had to be perfect. I made the best arrangements I could make, which included a chauffeur-driven limousine that picked us up at my home since we all lived within two miles of each other in Huntington, Connecticut.

We left Kennedy Airport in New York on September 7, bound for Vancouver, British Columbia. The next morning we flew into

Fort St. John and met Hank's son, Paul, who drove us to the ranch. Travel looked doubtful the next morning because of fog. The pilot finally said, "Let's give it a try." So Hank, the pilot and I climbed on board and took off. We tried to follow a river, but there was still too much fog forcing us to turn around and wait again. It looked awful doubtful that we would get into Keily Creek camp that day, let alone hunt the next. But the fog lifted some later that afternoon, allowing us to make it to camp that evening. The next morning it was snowing hard.

The plan of action was to separate to other camps. Monty and John left for the Red Fern Lake area, probably one of the prettiest areas in British Columbia, with its blue-green crystal clear mountain lakes and towering mountains rising approximately 8000-9000 feet. Arnold and I would hunt out of the Keily Creek camp for a few days and then move out to separate spike camps.

I spent the first seven days hunting moose. I turned down dozens during that time, waiting for a possible record-book entry. I had 15 days to hunt, why take a small one when there were so many to choose from? I finally shot a nice, symmetrical 48-incher on the eighth day. It wasn't as big as some of the bulls I had passed on earlier, but time was running out. Two of the bulls I saw were in the 55-inch range. I also passed up two bears that time. One was a real black bear, the other a small grizzly. The grizzly was heading away from us so I did not shoot. I've read too many stories on grizzlies to know that you don't shoot them in the butt. I did not want a mad, wounded bear on my hands.

Arnold, in the meantime, shot a nice moose on the first day of his hunt and on the third day, shot the biggest elk ever collected from the Keily Creek camp. Not bad — 2 animals, 3 days.

After collecting my moose, we decided to try for goats in High Keily, another camp area about a day's ride from camp. Before we left, we talked to another hunter in camp who had just returned from there. He told us where it was and where to check for bear or wolf sign. That little clear plastic tent sure looked and felt good after an eight-hour horseback ride in a steady rain. That night, the rain turned to snow. There were approximately four inches on the ground when we woke up.

After breakfast, we rode up the river valley a few miles looking for goats. We struck out, so we headed back to camp to try another area. On the way back, we found a large set of fresh grizzly tracks heading down the river towards our camp. When we got back to camp, I checked the moose kill and found that it had been moved.

Further investigation showed that the grizzly had dragged the remains approximately 25 feet. That alone, said something for the size of that old boy. I spent the next day waiting for the bear, but he never showed up. We rode back to the Keily camp the next morning. I figured the goats could wait until another year. I was going to concentrate on grizzlies for the rest of the hunt.

On the fourteenth day, we rode out to the area where Arnie had collected his moose to see if anything was eating on it. When we got to the top of a ridge about 450-500 yards from the kill, we dismounted and glassed the area. I immediately noticed something that looked furry. I quickly sat down and put my elbows on my knees to steady my 10x40 Zeiss glasses. That's when I first saw the bear. He was very dark colored, and lying in a ball, leading me to believe that he was asleep. I looked over at my guide and he motioned me to follow him. He wanted to stalk closer to get a better look.

The stalk ended when we were 75 yards from the bear. We still couldn't see much of him, but I did notice that the moose was nowhere in sight and the earth around the kill was all torn up as if someone had attacked it with a backhoe. I sat down while my Indian guide, Angus, stood behind me looking through his glasses. Angus told me to get ready because he was going to whistle, hopefully getting the bear to stand up so we could see him. I brought my Model 70 .300 Winchester Magnum up, centered it on the patch of fur that we could see and whispered, ''Ready.''

Angus whistled and the bear was on its feet in a flash, staring right at us. Angus hissed, ''Shoot! Shoot!'' but all I could see was a bigger mass of fur through the trees. ''I can't see his head!'' ''He's looking straight at us,'' hissed Angus again, this time with more urgency in his voice. ''Shoot!!!''

''I told you I can't see his head,'' I replied a little angrily this time. ''All I can make out is his left side.''

The bear ended the argument when he moved slightly, still trying to figure out what we were. It was all I needed. I put the crosshairs of my 3-9x Leupold under his left shoulder, figuring the 180-grain Remington soft point would go into the lung area. I touched it off. The griz dropped down on all fours and took off into the thick spruces behind him.

''You missed,'' said Angus shaking his head. I knew he was wrong. I shot from a solid sitting position and my sight picture was good. It was like shooting a sitting duck. We walked over to the area where the bear was standing and found a small patch of fur.

We also found out what happened to the moose! He had buried it completely! It's quite hard to believe an animal could become a backhoe. In the past number of years, I've read where if you're attacked by a bear, play dead and he'll bury you and then return a few days later to eat on you. They won't usually eat fresh killed meat and in this case it seemed true because this moose was 14 days old.

The snow made tracking very easy. It's hard to miss prints that are seven inches across and 11 inches long. Angus said by the looks of his prints and the quick flashes of him running through the spruces, it was the biggest bear he had ever seen. As we went from the small clearing to the thick spruces, I found a speck of very light colored blood. I turned to Angus, "Looks like a lung shot, all right. I didn't miss." I led the way into the spruces and found another glob of blood on the side of a small spruce shrub approximately three and a half feet above the ground, showing that I had hit him in the side. One step later, I spotted a small spruce about 25 feet in front of us start swaying back and forth !

All hell broke loose. The grizzly let out a growl that almost straightened out what little hair I have left. Angus yelled, "Let's get out of here!" I yelled back, "Don't shoot and back out slowly." Angus carries a .30-30 Winchester, which to me is entirely inadequate for stopping a charging grizzly. Angus and I backed into the clearing to discuss our next move. I already knew what Angus wanted to do...he wanted to run to the top of the ridge and wait. And wait we did, for three hours, arguing the entire time about what to do next. Angus wanted to head back to camp and wait until morning before checking up on the bear. I didn't like the idea of leaving a wounded bear in the woods, even though there were no other hunters other than myself in the area. The thought of losing him also worried me. I finally gave in and we left to return the next day with possibly another guide to help with the search if the bear wasn't dead. It started snowing hard as we rode back to camp and all I could think of was losing the bear's tracks.

That afternoon, Hank sent in Johnny Big Foot, another guide, who was coming off a 15-day sheep hunt that I originally requested. That evening at dinner, we talked about how big the bear was, the size of his prints in the snow, how he buried the remains of Arnie's moose and naturally, the growl. Everyone tried to cheer me up by saying, "Don't worry, he'll be there in the morning—if he's hit like you say he is."

Wes Blakeman's grizzly was so big that his first guide, who was carrying a .30-30 Winchester, turned and ran when the wounded bear threatened to charge. One shot from Wes' .300 Winchester Magnum was enough to kill the monster.

The next morning, we were all at the breakfast table before daybreak, ready to challenge the world. It was a nice day, a little cold, but at least the snow had stopped. Before leaving, our camp cook, Hermann Berg, who was in charge of camp during Hank's absence, called me aside. He said I could extend my hunt if I wanted and have Johnny Big Foot for my guide. I told him I would like Johnny to come along after the bear and if the bear was dead there was no problem, but if it was gone, I would like him to take Angus' place.

We reached the area where the bear was last seen after a 10 or 12 mile ride. Angus, this time on horseback, led the way, Johnny was next and I brought up the rear. From the top of the horses you could, in places, see down through the spruces. Approximately 30 to 40 yards in, Angus yelled that he could see the bear. It was dead.

We all dismounted and quickly went in to check my trophy. All we could say to each other was, "What a monster!" Johnny said that in his 23 years of guiding he had never seen one that size. Naturally, that made me even happier. We took some pictures after cutting a number of spruce trees that were in the way. It took all three of us to roll the bear into position.

Johnny and Angus skinned the bear while I built a large fire to let them warm their hands every now and then. It took them about two hours to skin the bear. After rolling the skin and head in a tarp, we tied it on my horse and left for camp, taking turns walking. Arriving in camp, everyone came to see if we had gotten the monster. After more picture-taking and story-telling, we settled down for a good night's sleep, especially since I was scheduled to leave in the morning. My 15-day hunt was over.

The next morning, the twin engine Islander was right on schedule. On board with the pilot was Hank and his wife, coming in to check everything out in camp. After hearing my story and seeing my bear's skull and hide, he also said it was the largest bear he had ever seen. I said good-bye to new-found friends and left for Fort St. John, a one hour flight. Weather was beautiful and I thought how peaceful it was here compared to back home. Unspoiled land, no high-rises, condos, and even better, no factories to pollute these beautiful lakes and streams; everything as it's been for centuries. God's country!

A few months after my hunt, I received a card from the British Columbia Fish & Wildlife Branch informing me that my bear was 19 years old. Another letter from Hank Foley and the British Columbia Outfitters Association informed me that my bear was the largest taken in British Columbia in 1984. Angus Davis received a silver belt buckle and Hank got a plaque for his wall. Me, I have the full mount of the bear standing to remind me of my hunt. I also have memories. The shaking of that little spruce tree and that growl will stay with me forever.

18

A Worthy Whitetail

by Dale Clayton

I have been hunting deer in Iowa with the traditional shotgun for a number of years and have had real success, including a 12-pointer shot in 1964 that scored 160-plus Boone & Crockett points. But there's a monster out here we call "Bullwinkle." A deer so big that some hunters in the area think it is as big as a moose.

I began bowhunting deer, including Bullwinkle, several years ago with my close friend and fellow NAHC member, Dennis Ridnour, also of Glenwood, Iowa. During that time, we have built numerous tree stands, both permanent and portable, trying our best to position ourselves correctly with all respect for wind, thermal currents, and of course, habits of the herd we try to intercept on the private land we hunt.

Nearly every weekend during the fall of 1983, from October to December, when our shotgun season starts, I had been perched in a tree or just leaning on one waiting for a fine trophy animal to come along. Things didn't go too well at first. I knew there was a good number of deer in the area, but during the early weeks of hunting season the signs just were not there. In mid-November I decided to break from my traditional hunting areas to find more promising signs of a large deer. The rut was on, so finding a good scrape or rub to hunt near wasn't difficult. I found a pine tree nearly six inches in diameter that literally had been ripped open, up

When Dale Clayton arrowed this 12-point Iowa buck, he already knew it wasn't "Bullwinkle," but he didn't care. Most hunters wouldn't!

and down its trunk. I built a temporary tree stand nearby and returned home with my spirits lifted. I felt I had a chance at bagging a big buck; what else could do so much damage to a tree that size?

Two days later I decided to return to that stand. Early the morning of November 18th, I thought I was positioned in the proper direction for an on-coming deer. I was wrong. A real nice eight-point buck suddenly appeared out of nowhere and, of course, from the wrong direction for me to take a good shot. I returned to the stand the next afternoon. The wind wasn't blowing exactly the way I wanted, so I applied extra scent to my incoming path.

It worked. Shortly after getting settled in the stand, a huge 12-point whitetail appeared about 50 yards away; right in the middle of the path where I had approached. It wasn't Bullwinkle, but it was definitely big! The scent I used must have been perfect, for he followed it up the path I had laid out to within 12 yards of my tree stand.

The combination of a Browning X-Cellerator, aluminum arrows and 4-Blade Savora heads did the trick. The long hours in the tree stand paid off, but the shot and the quick trailing job went too fast. It seemed too easy.

But even with this one under my belt, the next one may not be any easier. Bullwinkle is still out there somewhere, and I'd like to get him next.

19

German Flier Hunts BC Goats

by Hubert Stoffel

I am a German Air Force Officer married to a "Michigan Girl." We have two children. I am currently on a three-year tour of duty as a flight instructor for young German fighter pilots. We train at George Air Force Base in the Mojave Desert along with the U.S. Air Force. Eventually, I will retire with my family in the United States because I feel you have more freedom in your great country than in the crowded "Old World."

Besides my tour of duty I consider my stay here an excellent opportunity to hunt the great North American continent. My hunting background is German all the way, that means traditional and fair chase orientated. Hunting North America to me means hunting wide open spaces in mostly undisturbed habitat for species that we don't get to hunt in my home country. I have an eye especially on native goats, sheep, bears, pronghorn and moose.

As soon as I knew about my U.S. tour of duty, I started studying books about North American big game and checking into outfitters. I wanted to hunt goats and sheep since they are demanding species to collect. Reading more about goats and their demanding environment, I was fascinated with them and finally settled for a goat, bear and moose hunt with Coast Mountain Outfitters in British Columbia.

To prepare for the hunt I ran, bicycled and lifted weights three times weekly, and shot about 50 rounds of ammo per month at the local shooting range. The rifle I had chosen for the hunt was a Brown Precision stocked Remington Model 700 .300 Winchester Magnum. The ammo I settled on was a hot, 180-grain Nosler Partition handload which gave me an honest 3100 feet per second.

It was September when I flew to Prince Rupert, British Columbia, and met with Bob Milligan, the outfitter, and my guide, 21-year-old Jason Burnett from Stewart. The flight to Allister Lake, a sidearm of the Skeena River, was a great introduction to the beautiful mountain scenery we were going to hunt. The weather was clear and warm and stayed that way throughout most of my hunt.

After landing and setting up camp, we took a short excursion to look for bears near a creek filled with spawning salmon. The splashing salmon, thick alder brush and very large black bear tracks got me stimulated for things to come. I even saw my first wild bear.

The next day was spent glassing goats, mostly nannies and kids, but also some very large billies. The lake was nearly sea level, but the surrounding mountains of snow and ice reached up to 7,500 feet—and that's where the goats were.

The next morning was spent glassing for goats again. We finally spotted a big billy about 9:00 in the only glacier area that Jason gave us a chance to reach. Our only chance was to climb up to the saddle along the creek that came from the glacier, almost a vertical slope, because crawling through the alder brush was impossible.

I have done some mountain climbing in the German Alps while hunting chamois, but it wasn't anywhere near as tough as this was. More than once Jason had to pull me up with his hands or rifle stock. One wrong step and my wife would have collected my life insurance.

By noon, we were only half way up the saddle. By 2:00 we were close to the saddle and beginning our final stalk. Jason found the billy on the other side of the saddle about three-quarters of a mile above the treeline. That gave me my strength back. We had to keep below the treeline to stay out of sight of the goat. There was no easy way to come from above.

It was after 4:00 when we finally reached our destination—but the goat was nowhere in sight. I was totally out of breath, so Jason told me to stay put while he went to look for the goat. A few minutes later, he got my attention by pointing to the glacier. It took me a few seconds to spot the goat climbing at a steady pace up the

Hubert Stoffel with his hard-earned goat. At this moment the hard work and aching knees are forgotten as the hunter enjoys the moment.

slope. I laid down, settled my rifle on my backpack and put the crosshairs of my 3-9X Zeiss about five inches below his shoulder blade. I estimated the range at 200 yards. When I squeezed the trigger the goat dropped and slid down the rocks about 20 feet. My shooting practice paid off!

The goat had a beautiful, long-haired winter coat and horns that measured about 9 inches. Jason said it would score just shy of the record book. It later scored 46⅜.

It took Jason 30 minutes to skin the goat and pack the meat for the descent. It took us seven and a half hours to get up the mountain, but only two and a half to get down.

But it wasn't easy. From top to bottom, we slid through alder brush and under log jams. Half way down, I couldn't feel my legs anymore. I wanted to stay right there and not move one more muscle. Jason, who had to pull me up, now had to drag me down.

Just before dark we reached the creekbed at the foot of the mountain. Thirty minutes later we were in camp, exhausted, but happy. My knees were swollen to double their normal size, and my arms and legs were badly scratched. But I had the trophy and the hunting adventure I had always dreamed of. I had earned my goat but without the help and expertise of my young guide, it would have been impossible.

A few days later, I took a big black bear near the creek. It was a perfect way to end the perfect hunt.

20

Father And Son Hunt For Alaskan Moose

by Craig Courtright

It was the 10th of August when James and I boarded the MV Leconte and departed Sitka, Alaska for three adventuresome weeks exploring the interior of our state. James, my 16-year-old son, had spent the summer working for the National Park Service salting away his earnings so that he could come along. The trip to Haines up the Inside Passage would take almost 24 hours. We were anxious to get there and get on the road.

For me, this trip was the second of a lifetime desire to see Alaska and partake of its wonders. As a District Ranger with the U.S. Forest Service, I have been fortunate in that I have been able to work in some of the most spectacular National Forests in Idaho and Montana. My current assignment as District Ranger on the 1.5 million acre Sitka Ranger District has been the icing on the cake. My son and I have spent many hours testing the local fishing and hunting. It certainly is a thrill to have a 35-pound king salmon or a 75-pound halibut tugging on your line.

All this tends to spoil a person, but I still found myself longing to see the interior and explore its resources. My first hunting trip to the interior took place in August, 1984. I was fortunate enough to go along with three experienced Dall sheep hunters on a backpack sheep hunt into the Chugach Mountains. The Chugach Range is one of the more rugged mountain ranges in Alaska and it harbors some of the better sheep hunting. It was a truly spectacular trip and tested all four of us to the maximum. I was successful in bagging a nice 1⅛ curl, 38-inch trophy ram. This trip was followed by a week on the Alaskan Peninsula hunting caribou, another successful hunt.

After that, I was hopelessly hooked on hunting in the interior. This was much to the chagrin of my wife who has patiently put up with this mania for the last 18 plus years of our marriage. And true to the cause, I have now gotten my son headed down the same path. Hunting locally for blacktail deer and listening to story after story was more than the poor kid could handle and that explained his presence on the 1985 expedition.

We arrived in Anchorage on August 19th and tied in with Virgil Henke and his father, Leland. Weeks before we had planned this rendezvous as the beginning of a long awaited moose hunt north of Kotzebue, Alaska. Kotzebue is located on the northwest coast of Alaska just south of the Brooks Range. Virgil is an experienced moose hunter and fellow employee of the Forest Service. James and I were still novices to moose hunting and had high hopes that Virgil would be the ticket to a successful hunt. During my years in Idaho and Montana, I had religiously applied for a moose permit every year but was never successful in the draw. Needless to say, I was really psyched for this trip.

We spent August 20th getting our gear packed for the flight the next day. True to the occasion, a lot of lies were told during the process, mainly for the edification of my son. The plan was to board a jet for Kotzebue the next day and tie in with Jim Rood, our bush pilot. We made it to the airport by 9:00 a.m. and were depressed by the heavy rain that started our day. Much to our disappointment, our flight to Kotzebue was canceled. We waited around the airport for hours and finally got on a rescheduled flight to Kotzebue that afternoon. It was late afternoon when we arrived. Our pilot was to have met us hours earlier and consequently had made other plans when we didn't show. The long and the short of it was we weren't going to get out that day—or the next two. Bad weather kept our flight plans on hold and it wasn't until late afternoon on Friday, August 23rd that we finally had everyone into our camp on a tributary to the Naotak River in the Miayumerac Mountains. We spent the remainder of the day moving our gear from the river gravel bar landing strip to a campsite in a stringer of black spruce timber.

We started seriously hunting on Saturday. We had seen a number of nice moose on the flight in, so we knew there were some big bulls in the area. That afternoon we spotted two large bull moose bedded in a swale across the river and about two miles below camp. These two old boys seemed content to stay put and chew their cud for awhile, so we planned a stalk to bag them both.

James and I headed down the river on the camp side to work below the moose and close in on them from the downriver side. Virgil and his dad crossed the river at the campsite and proceeded toward the moose from the upriver side. Our plan was to catch the two bulls in a squeeze play, and bag them close to the river where we would have an easier pack to a river bar landing area. It was not as easy as it may sound as the moose were about 50 feet above the level of the river and had a good view of the countryside around them. All of us had to make good use of the available cover and stalk with utmost patience. James and I had a real scare when we accidentally spooked a cow moose. Fortunately, she went away from the two bulls, not alerting them to our presence. We crossed the river below the bulls and crawled up the river bank through the willow brush to a low ridge overlooking the moose. We were within 75 yards of the bulls.

The waiting game began. We had agreed to let Leland have the first shot at the largest bull. The adrenalin was really pumping those last few minutes as we knew we had the two bulls dead to

rights. Both were real trophies too, with one in the 60-inch class.

Virgil and Leland finally jumped the bulls and both shot at the larger bull but missed. Sometimes you get lucky and in this case the larger of the two bulls dived off the river bank and then turned uphill coming right at me. I put the first 250-grain Norma slug from my Ruger M77 .338 Winchester Magnum into his brisket between the shoulders. I distinctly remember the loud wack of the bullet as it hit the bull. The old boy acted like nothing had happened! I chambered a fresh round and put another slug through his shoulders with another loud wack. It sounded like someone was swatting the bull with a big paddle and that's about how he acted. I had been told that moose don't know when they are dead and it was certainly the case here. I had scored with two lethal hits in a matter of less than a minute before he reached the edge of the tundra and finally laid down. When I approached him, he still had his head up and I dispatched him with a round to the base of the skull.

The other bull was also a tough critter and actually charged Virgil after several lethal hits. He was dispatched with one final shot. Virgil's bull later measured 50 inches even; mine 64½.

It was late early evening and we had two nice bull moose down and a lot of work ahead of us. The excitement and satisfaction of making my dream come true made the butchering less of a chore. We had the meat boned-out, sacked and hauled to a river bar landing area about a quarter of a mile down-river by 11:00 p.m. We laid the meat sacks out on the bar and covered them with cut willows to allow proper cooling. We made it back to camp about midnight.

The next few days were spent lounging around camp, glassing the countryside for sheep and caribou. We also got in some fishing for some real nice grayling and arctic char. The grayling were running 16 to 18 inches and the char up to five pounds. After several days of this, my son was ready to make a try for his first Dall sheep. We headed upriver to hunt the mountainside we had seen sheep on for several days. It was late afternoon when we got to our crossing and the weather was getting bad. We had been plagued with constant showers during the entire hunt, but our time living in Sitka had taught us to go for it, rain or shine. We took refuge in a dense stand of aspen, birch, and black spruce on a nearby river bar and waited out a downpour. We had found a large open grown spruce under which we cached a large supply of dead wood making a combination shelter and woodpile. This was to

Because his bull was still in velvet, Craig Courtright's bull missed making the record book by 14 points.

prove worthwhile later that day.

When the rain stopped, it was already 5:00 p.m., but we had a lot of daylight left and could make it up to the sheep in about a 1½ hour climb. We went for it. About 8:00 p.m., we encountered our first ram, a young ¾ curl. As ⅞ is the legal minimum, we moved on to look for more. An hour later we spotted another band of sheep, and this one had a legal ⅞ curl in it. I had the ram in my sights, but wanted James to have a chance at him. I ducked back around the ridge to see my son standing up looking toward the sheep. I motioned him to get down for about the one thousandth time and was hopeful that the sheep hadn't seen him. Sheep are extremely wary and don't ever give you a second chance. Thinking that the sheep hadn't seen James, we made a very careful stalk to get a closer shot. Thirty minutes later, I peeked over a ridge expecting to see five sheep bedded nearby, instead seeing five rear ends headed away with about 600 yards between us. I couldn't believe what I was seeing as the sheep had given no inclination of having seen me earlier. What I didn't know was that my son had seen a full-curl ram higher up and this sheep had also seen him. He hadn't shot at that ram as I had explicitly told him not to shoot until I had given clearance. It's not always easy to tell a legal sheep until you've seen a few up close and I didn't want any mistakes. In the thrill of the chase, James had forgotten to tell me about the larger ram. We headed off the mountain, disappointed but still appreciative of the experience of getting close to the sheep.

All was not lost, however. On the way down, we walked up on a herd of about 40 caribou and James shot his first caribou. I also had a chance, but missed a long shot at a big bull. We boned out James' young bull, filled our packs and headed back to our shelter on the river. We made it just in time for another downpour.

In the morning, I noticed that my boots were looking a little funny, as the soles were shaped like the keel of a john boat. However, being tired and focusing on getting back to camp, I paid it no attention until I tried to put them on my feet. My size 11s had shrunk to size eight! I had put my wet boots too close to the fire overnight, and they had dried out. Not being one to let those things get the best of me, I did some creative leather carving, removing most of the shrunken hard leather. This almost reduced the boots to soles, leaving only the soft interior leather and the heavy outer leather along the back, the toe and the tongue. I managed to hobble back to camp in these podiatric wonders.

We lounged around camp the remainder of that day, periodically going down river to check our moose meat cache. We were expecting our pilot to pick up the meat that day, but weather had him grounded in Kotzebue. We covered the meat that night and gave the sacks a good sprinkling of pepper to discourage predators. It was stormy that night with heavy rain and a lot of wind. It was very noisy, and we didn't hear the grizzly that came into camp and pulled all of the caribou meat out of the tree about 50 yards from the tent. The bear consumed about 60 pounds of boned out meat, leaving only torn sacks and rope.

We were concerned about our meat cache down the river and were tracking the grizzly when our pilot came in. We met him on the river bar strip and got the dreaded news. The bear had found it too. We went down there right away and managed to salvage half the meat and the two sets of antlers. Our pilot came back that afternoon and was able to get the meat, antlers and Leland and my son back to Kotzebue before dark. Virgil and I stayed that night and subsequently got weathered in for two more days.

21

Handgunning for Cougar

by Fred Markley

I had come 600 miles, wallowed through chest-high snow drifts, climbed toward peaks that soared to 13,000 feet and suffered such exhaustion that it threatened to take my rib cage apart.

But none of it mattered anymore, as I stood at the base of a massive Ponderosa pine and stared at the largest cougar I had ever seen. My guide and his hounds waited quietly for me to make the next move. I reached down to my hip and touched the butt of my .357.

As a cop in the small community of Carpinteria, California, just 10 miles south of Santa Barbara, I handle my .357 daily. So I thought it more fitting that this moment be shared with it than any one of the dozen rifle/scope combinations that I had in my gunrack back home.

The cat was less than 20 yards away. A simple shot from a flat angle. Had the cat been a paper target, I might have tried a hip shot at it just for fun; but the scramble that had taken my wind and my ethics as a sportsman disallowed such foolishness. A 20-yard shot is as easy to miss as one at 50 yards. Yet, I was confident. It was time. The silence of the snowbound wilderness of southern Utah was only broken by an impatient whine from one of the hounds.

This hunt began with an outdoor magazine ad which read: "Lion/Bear Hunts." Dave Handrich, guide and outfitter, was the man. I learned that Handrich used only the finest Walker dogs. To

Dave's credit was the fact that his hounds had treed the largest of the big cats in years. Best of all, Dave lived only 10 miles away in Santa Barbara.

Dave Handrich would stand out in a crowd at six-feet two-inches, about 180 pounds in wet boots. No fat about his belt, his handsome, leathered face, battered cowboy hat, jeans and western boots all completed the image.

I arrived at Dave's camp near Cedar City, Utah, after I had been at the wheel for nearly 11 hours. I was a full day ahead of schedule, but it gave me some time to wander about his camp and admire the efficiency of his setup. He had horses, snowmobiles and all the equipment to make a complete and thoroughly efficient expedition into the rough country that is sometimes called "Little Dixie," because a number of settlers from the South came to Utah following the Civil War to escape Sherman's March to the Sea.

A camping trailer was ready for me and my equipment, so I transferred my gear from the car to my temporary home. The Dave Handrich I met in Santa Barbara had become another man with the Rockies at his back. No Gary Cooper doled out the "yeps" and "nopes" any better than Dave. And when he did open up, he said things in fewer words than most.

We left camp early the next morning with the temperature at four degrees above zero. The canyons we worked showed no cat tracks. In fact, we didn't find any cat sign until 3:00 p.m. the second day. Dave asked me if I wanted to run it, explaining that we might be out after dark if we turned the dogs loose. Follow the hounds through deep after dark? You bet! I had not come this far to stay warm and dry.

The next several hours were spent running in belly-deep powder snow, the type skiers spend a year's wages to play in. The wisdom of Dave's suggestion began to soak in along with the realization that I had felt no sensation in my feet for several hours. We spent what seemed to be a lifetime floundering up canyon after canyon trying to find the dogs. We gave up and headed back to the truck to wait for them. It was a cold miserable night there in the cab and the dogs did not return until early morning. I was a heck of a lot wiser when we finally got back to camp nearly 24 hours after we left.

Time whisked by after that, but no lion was to be found. Too soon it was the morning of the fourth day. We decided to work a canyon somewhat closer to camp. We knew it was a long shot, but we were getting desperate. Ironically, Dave hadn't gone 200 yards

from the truck when he found some "sure enough" cougar tracks, big tracks that had to be made by a large male. He came back waving his arms and hollering, "Cougar, cougar!" We quickly gulped down a lunch knowing that it could be another 24 hours before we got back. Meanwhile, the dogs had been set loose and their song warbled into the foothills. They were singing "hot track," but Dave and I knew that "hot" and "treed" were two different songs.

With a few hours head start, the cat, an old and wise one, tested the dogs with a few of the preliminary devices that can make cougar hunters give up and sell pencils on street corners. There was a bit of sheer cliff-side maneuvering along an icy slope to see if the dogs were sincere. Then he took them through a tangle of rock-slides and windfalls that would have discouraged a snake.

I couldn't keep up, so Dave and the dogs left me behind. Adding to the agony of my shredded nerves and exhausted body was an attack of diarrhea. I was belly deep in the snow and steam rose from my shoulders as I exerted myself to push ahead and think positive.

I followed the trail for five hours, before I heard the dogs barking "treed." But the sight of the cat in a 70-foot Ponderosa made it all worthwhile.

Dave was standing as quietly as one of the trees when I finally caught up to him. He knew, as well as I, what I had to do. I scrambled up the opposite slope and the cat was straight across from me. No artist could have posed the tremendous creature in a more dramatic stance; hind feet balanced lightly on one massive limb as its front paws rested at a higher level. It breathed lightly having been up long enough to have rested. My breaths came in gasps.

Thoughts raced through my mind. I remembered the pronghorn I'd taken back in '64 that missed the NRA Silver Bullet Award by ⅝ of a point. Then there was the javelina that placed second in Arizona's all-time list. Now I had the king of them all in front of me.

The orange-tinted sights of the magnum brought my nerves under control. They rested just under the cat's vitals and a voice from a thousand pistol matches said, "Breath a little, let it out and squeeze."

The magnum rocked in my hand. There was no way to miss. Yet, the cat merely looked for a higher limb after the Model 19 sent a 158-grain SJHP into the branch where it stood. Dave

Success on the second shot tagged this record book lion for Fred Markley.

shouted for me to shoot again—quick! He knew that if the cat was creased, it would kill the dogs when they charged.

I saw it jump for another branch. I immediately lined up the sights and squeezed off another round just as the cat leaped into the snow below. The dogs were after it in a flash.

"Did you hit him at all?"

"Yea," I said. "I know I hit him." But I felt more like sinking into the earth.

I knew that Dave had done his homework on me as well as me on him. Taking a prospect into the mountains to hunt was one thing; but taking one to hunt with a handgun is something else. He had taken me because I had seemed like an experienced hunter and gunman, and now I had missed a full-grown mountain lion at 20 yards.

As Dave ran down the canyon after the dogs, I ran after him. The snow was hip deep and my adrenalin was all that kept me going; yet, Dave left me as though he were on showshoes.

Ahead, we heard the dogs baying once more. I prayed that they would not get cut up by the wild cat, but it wasn't necessary. The cat was dead. It lay as though it had decided to sleep off a nightmare of men and hounds which had plagued it all day long.

I could hardly believe the size of the cat; neither could Dave. A magnificent male, the cougar was in excellent condition, except for a few scars from fighting over the ladies. Its massive chest and stocky formation made it special. The pads were the size of a man's hand. It was seven feet, three inches long and weighed 161½ pounds. The second largest Dave has ever treed in Utah.

We skinned the cat and found a single hole in the right side. The Speer CCI bullet had cut through one rib and centered in the heart. My first shot had dimpled a limb in the 70-foot Ponderosa.

Later, in Santa Barbara, Dave called to let me know the cat was the largest taken all year from his camp, 15 pounds heavier than the next best.

The scoring of a cougar skull is delayed 60 days, during which time the skull drys before measuring. Hugh Roodom, an official measurer with Boone and Crockett, scored it 15¹⁄₁₆. The skull measured 9¹⁄₁₆ inches long by six inches wide. My cat, which ranks 126th in the 1981 Edition of the Boone & Crockett record book, has been mounted life-size.

22

My Own Knife
Almost Took My Life

by Steve Schaust

I have been a member of the North American Hunting Club, and a bunch of other organizations, for years, so I've been reading about big game hunts for a long time. But I really got the itch to make the dream come true about 1980. My dream finally became reality in 1983, but the reality was more of a nightmare.

Of all the places I wanted to hunt, Alaska held the most intrigue. Beautiful caribou, enormous moose, magnificent Dall rams, splendid mountain goats, fierce bears and many more game animals than I have adjectives to describe. The only problem was that a guided hunt cost more than I could afford as a Minneapolis X-ray technologist. I knew I would have to cut corners somewhere, but the problem was "How?" I found that answer during the two years of researching and planning my dream hunt. I discovered plenty of ways to cut costs and still enjoy a quality hunt. The biggest dollar savings, was not to hire a guide but to hunt entirely on my own. I realized that it's best to have a hunting partner, but being young and in fairly good shape, I figured I could make do without one. Besides, I had considerable solo hunting experience in the lower 48, and enjoy hunting by myself.

In Alaska, you can't hunt Dall sheep or brown and grizzly bears without a guide. That still left me with many options. My Number One priority was a good-size caribou. After that, I wanted a moose, a mountain goat, and possibly a black bear. And, as long as this was a dream hunt, I listed other possibilities such as blacktail deer and other game offered on special permit hunts.

With all this in mind, I planned to go where the Boone and Crockett record book said the most caribou trophies came from in Alaska—the Alaskan Peninsula—but I had to plan to catch the migration.

I left some details open-ended to allow for side trips for other game if I was successful with my top priority trophies. Central and southwestern Alaska seemed good for big moose, and isolated areas along the southern coast and the southeastern panhandle looked good for big mountain goats, according to information I received from the Alaska Fish & Game Department. I based my tentative side trips on good trophy areas that were also accessible to a do-it-yourselfer like myself.

The easy part was packing up the gear, including a Remington Model 700 BDL .30-06 and a "bear back-up" 870 Wingmaster 20 gauge, which could also feed me daily if I could hit ptarmigan and other delectable small game. The Bushnell Trophy spotting scope, a 16x36X model, was as valuable as the hip boots I wore during 95 percent of the hunt.

The tough part was juggling my schedule, swapping days and taking vacation to come up with a total of two months away from work. When that fell into place, I packed up my Ford four-wheel-drive with camping and hunting gear and began my trek.

The long drive ended in Fairbanks, where I visited friends. I followed it with a quick trip to Valdez to try for goat. The dangerous snow, ice and bad weather opened my eyes to the "do-it-yourself dangers" and I think I was wise to pack it in early, and retreat from the lone goat routine.

Reports on the caribou migration said the herd was a bit behind schedule, so I filled the gap with three days of unsuccessful black bear hunting. My lack of success was quickly eroding my enthusiasm for my solo safari. My hopes now were riding on moose as I joined my friends from Fairbanks for a hunt near Paxson in east-central Alaska. Three-wheel ATV's took us deep into the bush.

It took me a week to finally catch up with a 40-inch bull, but the .30-06 was gun enough to bring him down without much trouble. A thousand pounds of moose is no joking matter, but my buddies from Fairbanks chided me about the rack. Seems they're used to five-foot spreads up there, but Minnesotans can appreciate the hunt no matter what the size of the antlers, at least I had them believing it long enough to let me continue my hunt.

With a moose under my belt now and my success just starting, I decided it was time to try for my first choice animal of this Alaskan adventure, a big bull caribou.

I drove to Anchorage and hopped a flight with Air Alaska to King Salmon, from which I took Peninsula Airways about an hour south, where I set up base camp. You better believe I remembered the signal for distress would be an orange tarp spread on the ground after that Cherokee 6 left me alone on a short stretch of sand in the wilderness.

Three Wyoming hunters who had used the base camp the week before I did, flew out with the pilot who flew me in. They had two caribou, but said the animals were pretty scarce. I should have known this wouldn't be the most comfortable experience by the way these guys were so anxious to leave.

If only the caribou would come as thick as the hordes of bugs. Every time I breathed I inhaled a mouthful of critters. A headnet and Muskol saved me as I set up camp near a small river close to the make-shift landing strip. A flock of swans discussed where they were going to land as they flew over, and the whole flood of new sights and sounds drowned me in a sea of awesome delight.

Sleep came hard, as big bull caribou fell to my gun with each of the 40 winks I stole within my sleeping bag. Wolves howled, serenading me into insomnia.

For days, I slept very little, glassed a lot, but saw only a few distant caribou and a couple of far off brown bear; thank the Lord for *far off* brown bear. That's one animal I quickly and easily gained respect for in the wilderness. One day, as I was spotting game, a big brown mass filled my scope. I grabbed for my rifle and jerked my head up at the same time, but no bear was in sight. I sat ready for minutes—long, long minutes. Then, I saw him, a porcupine on the little hill in front of the spotting scope. My heart stopped pounding a few minutes later.

Days passed, and the monotony and disappointment of more caribou, but few racks, finally got to me. Wind and rain beat me and the long stalks that ended in no shot because the racks were too small, all take their toll. Ptarmigan stew was somewhat satisfying, but when I was cleaning the pots the next morning real satisfaction arrived. Across the river was a nice herd of maybe 100 caribou with at least a dozen big bulls. They were over the next ridge before I could stop staring at the huge racks. I grabbed some candy, my boots and a rifle. I'm diabetic, so the candy helps maintain my blood sugar.

They were always one ridge ahead of me. I tried to catch up, but didn't have enough energy. But I wasn't going to give up. Ten ridges and four rivers later, I caught up with them.

The caribou were feeding in a little basin about 150 yards from the ridge I was on. I immediately sized up the bulls. The adrenalin really started flowing when I noticed five of the bulls near the back of the herd had impressive double shovels. Deciding which one to take was tough. I finally picked one I thought looked the biggest and took a deep breath. The crosshairs came into place and I waited for the shuffling herd to clear. I wanted to make sure another caribou wasn't behind my bull because I knew the 180-grain Federal Premium load could do its job and still push the Nosler Partition bullet into another animal. Usually, though, it mushrooms just right to do the trick inside the game. I just wanted to be extra careful before taking the shot.

I squeezed the trigger. The sound spooked the herd toward the next ridge. My bull was with them. I lost track of him and couldn't get another shot. But it didn't matter because my bull soon lagged behind enough for me to finish him off with a second shot.

I was standing over him in no time. I cleaned him up and started to cape out the hide, all the while admiring the sure record book rack. That's when I made a near fatal mistake.

I exerted a little too much pressure on my knife and drove the blade through the caribou's hide and deep into my thigh. It penetrated to the bone. I stood there, alone in the bush, with a bloody knife—my own knife—stuck in my leg.

Slowly, I eased the knife out, wincing from the pain, but strangely feeling in control. I was afraid the blood would come gushing out and the wolves would have a double treat waiting for them. The thick layers of skin and muscle slid back together, but fortunately the blood never flowed freely. Here's where my hospital emergency room training paid off. I knew from the lack of blood that I didn't have to panic for the moment because I had missed the major artery and veins. I wrapped a bandana around the wound as a pressure bandage and headed back for camp. Don't ask me what possessed me to do it, but I hauled those damn four-foot antlers on my shoulders as I hobbled back to camp. I guess I felt I deserved them, and I was either aware of the fact that the wound

Steve Schaust took on the Alaskan wilderness on his own to bag this truly beautiful caribou bull.

wasn't so serious or I must have figured if I was going to die, they would be my tombstone.

Well, I wouldn't be telling this if I didn't make it back to camp, but you can bet I was sore and tired like all get out. Happy to be "home," I stitched myself up with stuff from my first-aid kit, and put on some antibiotic salve.

I spent the next day hobbling back and forth bringing the rest of the caribou meat back to camp. I also put out the signal for the plane to pick me up on its daily pass to other camps. The next day, the pilot landed and looked at me like I had just been through World War III. I knew I had him confused because I was wearing a proud smile that can only be understood by those who matched wits with wild game in its own world and came home with more than memories as a tribute to the hunt.

The satisfaction was intensified after the hunt when my caribou scored 420 points, well above the 400-point minimum for the Boone and Crockett record book.

23

Try Tracking A Grizzly

by Enrico Ciaburri

A fter tracking the bear for three miles, I couldn't believe my eyes. The enormous grizzly was only 50 yards away. I raised my gun and found him in the scope, waiting for the guide to confirm my hunch. The word came. "Shoot!"

I was on my second grizzly hunt of the year. I had hunted the previous spring with my guide, and while we had spotted a number of grizzly, none were close to trophy size. I still had the bear hunting bug when my hunt ended, so when the guide explained that if I had enough patience and a lucky charm to go with it, we would stand a good chance of taking an exceptional bear during the fall season, I jumped at the chance.

Time seemed to be at a standstill the next few months. I exercised daily and even gave up smoking to condition myself for the upcoming hunt.

I flew into Anchorage on October 5. That evening, Pete, my guide, and I discussed our plans. He informed me that there had been a good snowfall in the vicinity of Big River, but he'd have to check weather conditions before flying. Big River is located east of McGrath, south of Farewell and drains into the Kuskokwin. The next morning, we flew out to the headwaters of Big river. As we were flying, I realized that Alaska was a land of immense beauty. I saw mountains and large river beds, and the setting was like a winter wonderland. We hit turbulence during the flight and I was

glad when we finally landed at the campsite.

I had trouble sleeping that evening because I was anticipating the days ahead. The next morning, we were up at the crack of dawn, but to our dismay, found sleeting conditions. It seemed like a stroke of bad luck.

After eating a quick breakfast, we put on our snowshoes and headed out. Fortunately, I had gained some experience using snowshoes while rabbit hunting in New York state. About a half-mile from camp, we came upon some bear sign along some sandbars. In the snow were tracks of a few medium-sized bears, but none of them were fresh. Heading on, we checked out some brushy areas. Moments later, my guide spotted some ravens circling ahead of us.

The ravens were feeding on a moose kill. Also feeding on the dead beast was a good-sized grizzly, if the size of the bear tracks surrounding the kill site were accurate. Pete thought it was a good idea to keep an eye on the kill as chances were good that the bear would return. We found a good place to sit and sat down, knowing full-well the day's agenda was already determined.

The cool wind and snow flurries made the wait uncomfortable, but we stuck it out until dark. Nothing showed the entire day, but Pete was undaunted. "I think we should head back there in the morning," he said as we headed back to camp in the dark. We settled into our sleeping bags soon after hearty helpings of caribou steak. That night I slept!

We set out for the moose kill at first light the next morning. When we got close enough, we glassed the entire area before approaching the site cautiously. Glancing down at the ground, I saw a huge set of bear tracks. My guide looked stunned!

The sight of those massive tracks sent my emotions soaring. "This is a real fresh track," Pete said as I knelt down beside him. "Let's see where he's headed!" We followed the track into the big timber. We must have hiked about three miles through the aspen and spruce covered terrain. Pete was cautious the whole way. He constantly surveyed the land ahead of us, watching for sign of the bear. One thing we didn't need was to be taken by surprise.

But we were! The huge grizzly was only 50 yards away when we finally spotted him as we topped a knoll. The giant instantly rose from his bed and looked at us, turning broadside in the process. He was overwhelming! I raised my .300 Winchester Magnum and put the crosshairs on his shoulder area. Pete whispered, "Shoot!"

My first shot bowled the bear over. All I could see was snow flying as the bear went down. Pete yelled, "Shoot again!" as the bear bounced back up and headed away from us. I found him in the scope again and yanked the trigger. He looked back in our direction, before moving into some brush to our left shaking his head as he went. My third shot dropped him.

My guide was even more excited than I was as we approached the bear after making sure he was dead. Pete said that this was the largest bear he had ever seen in all of his hunting career. After examining the huge bear, I was inclined to believe him. We took a number of photos and then skinned the bear. The pelt was thick, flawless and heavy. I couldn't believe how much it weighed. In order for us to carry it out, the skull and paws had to be skinned out to decrease the weight. Even then, it weighed close to 200 pounds!

When I returned home to New York, I had the skull scored after the 60-day drying period ended. It scored unofficially $27^{11}/_{16}$. This should make it the largest recorded. According to The Alaska Fish & Game Department, the bear was 16 years of age, putting him well past his prime.

24

New Jersey Beauty

by Bob Eisele

The day was clear and a hint of fall was in the air when I made my way from my truck to the trail that leads to my deer stand. I checked my gear and applied some Deer Formula scent to my boot pads and started my final sneak to my deer stand.

I actually started this hunt much earlier, during an early-winter hunt at the end of the previous season. I had seen a large set of deer tracks while bowhunting. Along about March, I started to scout the area in earnest. I found lots of old sign, such as old scrapes and rubs along a trail that was in a natural corridor of white oaks between a thick swamp and a green briar thicket.

Over the next few months, I made short scouting trips through the area to learn better the lay of the land. The area was ideal for hunting, having a swamp for cover and water, white oaks for food, and a sense of security as it was rather hard to get into.

During my scouting forays, I located an ideal location for a tree stand in a small stand of about six holly trees. Holly trees have green leaves year-round, so they would offer me good cover during the fall hunt. I positioned a portable ladder stand in the hollies, taking special note of which direction the prevailing winds were coming from. The stand was situated within 20 yards of where two trails crossed, doubling my chances. Things looked good.

On one of my trips through the area in early September with my wife Becky, I spotted the buck feeding along a trail that would take him right past my stand. We hid, not wanting to spook him, while his newly peeled antlers gleamed in the late-afternoon sun.

I spent the remaining weeks before the season opener practicing with my Browning Explorer bow which is set at 65 pounds. I shoot 2117 Easton Gamegetter shafts and Snuffer broadheads. I practiced from the ground and from a ladder stand I had erected in my back yard.

The bow season finally arrived in late-September, but the weather was still rather warm. I elected not to hunt my "holly stand" right away, but did make a few short hunts in a couple areas I had been scouting. I really don't like hunting the same area or stand two days in a row. Sometimes I use a stand only once a week. A trophy buck doesn't get that way by being dumb and I believe a buck will move out of an area if you hunt it too much. I only used my new stand twice before I got my buck. On one of my previous hunts in this stand, I had a spike buck and four does pass by.

The day I shot the buck, I noticed two fresh scrapes on my way into my stand, and once in it, I could see no less than nine more around me. The area was really hot. I was in the core of his breeding area, and I knew it was only a matter of time before he would show up.

When I reached my stand, I took off the foot pads that were soaked in the Deer Formula and dropped them about seven yards from the base of my ladder stand. I also put a few drops of red fox urine on the base of my ladder before climbing up.

The woods were beautiful and after a half an hour the birds and small animals were oblivious to my entrance, going about their business as usual. After two hours of soaking in my surroundings, I heard a slight rustle in the brush along the trail to the southeast. Shortly, a large doe came down the trail, stopping often to pick up acorns. She kept looking over her back tail, alerting me to the possibility that something was following her. I hoped that something was "my" trophy buck.

After what seemed like hours, I saw movement down the same trail. An animal was making its way down the trail towards me. Each step brought it closer. Finally, as if stepping into a spotlight, "my" buck—in all his splender—stepped into a shaft of sunlight, his polished antlers reflecting light rays like a mirror.

I nervously positioned myself for a shot. The buck would pass me at 10 yards if he continued to travel in the direction he was heading. It didn't turn out that way. Just as he approached the edge

Months of scouting and planning paid off for Bob Eisele when he bagged this 12-point New Jersey beauty.

of my shooting lane, a squirrel darted in front of him, causing him to jump back and run off about 45 yards. He stood there stamping his foot and scrutinizing the entire area. I almost passed out trying not to move! I kept hoping he wouldn't hear my heart pounding like a trip hammer or see the holly trees shaking!

He finally decided everything was okay and started back down the trail, only this time he had changed his route by a few yards. Lucky for me, he passed through the outer edge of my shooting lane—16 yards away.

I drew and shot. Much to my surprise, the buck dropped in his tracks! I didn't know what to do, so I sat there watching him for about five minutes. Satisfied that he was down for good I lowered my bow to the ground and climbed down to claim my prize. When I turned around, the buck was standing there watching me! He was gone before I could shoot.

I was dumbfounded. I didn't know what to do. I was afraid to move, but then I was also afraid not to move. So I did the next best thing—I sat down. I waited 30 long minutes before starting a slow but easy tracking job. I went about 50 yards in 20 minutes and found where the deer had fallen, but I didn't find him. I thought I had heard him moving off, so I sat down and gave him more time.

After another hour and a half, I continued on to find the deer piled up in a pine thicket just 60 yards ahead. I just sat there and admired the buck I had worked so hard to claim.

The buck was truly magnificent! A typical 6x6 with a 1½-inch sticker point on one back tine. He dressed out at 153 pounds and green-scored 148⅞ Pope & Young points. A New Jersey beauty!

25

Grizzlies,
Ice Storms and Caribou...

by Dan Hart

My caribou was taken on a Swap Hunt that was arranged through *Keeping Track*, making this adventure all the better. Bill O'Halloran, an Army helicopter pilot stationed in Fairbanks, Alaska, advertised a hunt for caribou, moose or black bear in exchange for elk, antelope or mule deer. I didn't call for quite a while because the expense just seemed too much for me to swing.

I had always dreamed of seeing Alaska, so I decided to call just to see what he had to say. After the first phone call, I was hooked. Right then I decided somehow, sometime, I was going to Alaska. The planning began.

The hardest part of the hunt was the waiting and saving money. Bill and I talked on the phone several times. He was trying to come up with a place to hunt caribou that wouldn't depend entirely on the migration and weather. I was running and exercising daily. I shot a couple of hundred rounds through my Sako 7mm Remington Magnum to come up with a good load using 160-grain Nosler Partition bullets. Finally I settled on 62 grains of IMR 4350 which put five shots in 1 inch at 100 yards.

One day Bill called and said I should probably cancel because the area he planned to hunt had been closed to nonresidents. For a couple of months, I thought the trip was over, but Bill called again and said he had found a place for us to hunt. I stepped up my exercise program and tore the rotator cuff in my right shoulder just a month before I was to leave. This was a very painful injury and once again I thought my trip was over. The doctor told me to go ahead, but to be careful.

Bill met me at the Fairbanks airport. In just a little while we were exchanging hunting stories like we had known each other for years. Bill is an enthusiastic hunter and I can't imagine anyone not liking him. We picked up my hunting licenses and went back to the airport in hopes my baggage had arrived on a later flight. Luckily it had.

The next morning we flew into our hunting area on the Little Delta River. Bill went in the first trip and I went second. It was a foggy and overcast day and I was worried about not getting in, but we didn't have any problems. Bill already had the small dome tent set up on the barren ridge where we landed the plane. As we flew in, I thought that this must be the most desolate camp in the world. The ridge we were on was gravel, dropping off sharply to the north and more gently into wet marshy tundra to the south. Through breaks in the clouds, I could see patches of high snow-capped mountains across the river. Our ridge ran about 4,000 feet, well above timberline.

Shortly after the plane left, it started raining. For the two weeks I was in Alaska, it rained or snowed every day except one. Bill and I donned our rain gear and started walking along the ridge, glassing off the steep incline to the north. Alaskan law doesn't allow shooting on the same day as flying, so that day we were just sightseers. We saw several caribou close to camp, but they were all cows and calves with an occasional small bull.

The first of the big bulls we spotted were in a bunch of seven that were browsing on a ridge about two miles from camp. They were still in velvet and they all looked awesome. I told Bill that anyone of them would be good enough for me. He chuckled, then assured me that there were bigger ones around. We spotted one of them an hour later and even Bill got excited. It was feeding along the top of the ridge with another bull. He was out of velvet and his double shovel crown looked enormous. We laid downwind of the bulls and they eventually fed to within 35 yards of us. Bill jumped up and threw rocks at them to make them run. I don't know of a sight that is more beautiful than that of a big bull caribou racing across the tundra with its rack swinging side to side.

Later that afternoon I spotted a big grizzly just below camp. We discussed the possibility of him coming into camp, but decided that only happens to other people. Just to be safe, we moved our garbage a couple of hundred yards from the tent and left our backpacks outside with the food.

About midnight, Bill elbowed me and hissed, "We've got a bear. He just growled right outside the tent." I laid still, planning to play dead if worse came to worst. Bill sat clutching his .44 Magnum. We never saw or heard any more of the bear. That was fine with me. The next morning Bill laughed and said, "It's all part of the Alaskan experience."

We left the tent early the next morning and didn't see any caribou where they had been the day before. Finally, I spotted one mediocre bull in a draw running up the side of the ridge. We sneaked around until we could see there were eight bulls in the bunch. Six of them were big!

We studied them through binoculars and a spotting scope. Any one of the six would make a fine trophy, but after seeing so many big bulls the day before, I was getting picky. We backed away from them and discussed the merits of each one and the possibility of getting a better one. After we had spent about an hour and a half looking around for others and waiting for them to come to the top of the ridge, the caribou bedded down. I decided to shoot the only double shovel bull in the group even though we would have to pack it up a steep hill. I sneaked around to within 60 yards of the group and shot the bull through the lungs.

The others ran around me and headed over the top of the ridge. Bill decided to shoot a bull with exceptionally nice bez points and a pretty gnarled top. He shot it the first time running at about 300 yards. The bull was hit too far back, but Bill followed him across the ridge and finished him in the wet tundra on the south side. He was also using a Sako 7mm Magnum, except he was using 175-grain Nosler Partitions.

I had followed Bill after his first caribou, so we got to his bull first. After many pictures, Bill put a tape on him. The main beams were 51 inches. Bill had underestimated his bull, so we figured mine was probably better than we first thought. He was. Both main beams measured over 60 inches and his best shovel was over 23 inches. We green scored him at 404½. Later, he officially scored 401½.

The work began. We boned my bull out and backpacked it to the top of the ridge. The ridge seemed to get steeper and steeper. By the last trip it seemed to be perpendicular. Fog rolled in and rain came with the cold wind. By the time we started working on Bill's caribou, the rain had started to freeze. It would hit our

Dan Hart persevered over "the Alaskan experience" to score on this caribou bull with his Sako 7mm Rem. Mag.

raincoats and freeze immediately. We had to keep our hands busy cutting meat because the meat was the only thing remotely warm. I had never been so cold in my life.

When we started packing the meat back to camp through the wet tundra, I discovered that you can work up a sweat while you think you're freezing to death. When we got back to the tent, the freezing rain was mixed with snow. We weren't even sure we could find the caribou again with the limited visibility so we crawled into the tent for the night. "All the bears should be holed up in this weather," I thought. At least I'll get a good night's sleep." I didn't.

About midnight, Bill woke me up by beating ice and snow off the tent with his flashlight. The wind was blowing so hard he was afraid we might lose the tent and that would probably be the end of us. I was beginning to think he just didn't like anyone to sleep all night.

I laid awake worrying about freezing to death instead of getting eaten by a bear. In the morning, Bill assured me again that it's all part of the Alaskan experience.

By morning, the weather had cleared except for a strong wind. We finished packing our meat to camp and spent the next two days glassing and laying around camp. In four days on the ridge, we saw about 2,000 head of caribou, three grizzlies, one black bear, one moose and four fox. The Alaskan experience was everything I dreamed it would be. I wouldn't have had it any other way.

26

Alberta Bighorn With A Bow

by Paul Izanti

The idea of hunting bighorn sheep came to me at the Foundation for North American Wild Sheep's annual convention. At the convention, I met different people and discussed hunting in different areas for other species of game. By talking with other hunters, I obtained a better idea of an individual outfitter's success than by talking directly to the outfitter. A satisfied hunter will give a person a better idea of what to expect. The name of Randy Babala was mentioned so often I had to search him out. My father hunted with Randy's uncle, Jim, in the 1960's and shot a big 183-point plus bighorn that made the Boone & Crockett record book. I was also hoping to take a ram that would score higher than Boone & Crockett's minimum of 180.

I have been a rifle hunter all my life and have taken lots of big game. The idea of bowhunting has always intrigued me, but up to that point I had never shot anything with a bow. So why did I gamble the chance of a lifetime on a piece of equipment that severely limited my effective shooting range and put me at an immense disadvantage against an animal reputed to have eyesight equivalent to 4x binoculars? I wanted to make my sheep hunt a real challenge, one that I would remember in my old age. The idea of being within bowrange of a majestic bighorn excited me beyond belief.

I did have one problem, though; I knew nothing about bows

and bowhunting. The first thing I did was contact my wife's cousin who is an avid bowhunter and asked him to go with me to purchase my bow. I am a left-handed shooter and found the Warthog B Magnum cam bow fit me like a glove. My cousin highly recommended aluminum shaft arrows and I chose Razorbak 5 broadheads, after reading several articles praising their performance.

Shooting practice started in early April and I practiced one hour per week until August. I wanted to practice more, but living in New York City I could only get away on weekends. My shooting form was very good so I was told only practice was going to help my shooting.

I met with Rick Guinn in Calgary and from his home we drove to Canamore where we met with Randy and John Groat. The following morning we packed all our gear into a pickup truck and drove to the starting point of the hunt. When we got there, we put on our packs and began the long climb. A novice at backpacking, I quickly fell behind and had to follow the others' tracks until I reached the camp site seven hours later. Sleep felt good that night.

After a hearty breakfast, we were off with our gear in day packs and bow in hand. We went up through a deep ravine above camp nicknamed Cougar Canyon. The snow was getting deeper making walking a little more difficult. Suddenly, Randy stopped and ducked behind a small pine tree, signaling me to hide also. We glassed ahead and I saw my first bighorn ram, a sharp three-quarters curl. Then more rams popped into view. There were seven in all, five of them legal, but the biggest was only about 36x15. I passed them up.

We continued upward, eventually breaking treeline. It began snowing lightly and it became difficult to glass any large area from one spot. We got into our white camo and proceeded uphill glassing as we went. We glassed several rams in high meadows and rock ledges, but none were big enough to meet the standards I had set. In all, we saw 18 rams and about 26 ewes, a good first day.

That night, we decided that spending more time in this area would be fruitless since we had covered most of it and hadn't seen the type of sheep I was looking for. Randy suggested that we move back down and try a different area. We did. In fact, we tried several different areas the next few days, but spotted only one ram that was close to the size I wanted and he was several hundred yards above us and moving higher. We decided to keep moving.

The following morning found all of us, Rick Guinn, Randy, John and myself hiking up Pigeon Mountain. It was bright and sunny but quite chilly. The snow on the south slopes was very deep and hard to walk in. When we stopped to eat, Rick told us that the rams in this range are known for 16 inch bases or better, so a good broomed 38-inch ram would be close to book size. While we ate, we glassed Mount Hood, site of the 1988 Olympic skiing events.

We got our first break when we circled a peak soon after lunch. Randy spotted some sheep and left us to investigate. When he returned, he had a half smile on his face. "There are nine rams and two look real good," Randy said, "but they are in the middle of a big meadow. The big rams might go 180 or a little better."

"Let's go," I said.

Most of the rams were feeding when we returned to the meadow Randy had found. One of the rams was very close to book size and I wanted a crack at him. A quick stalk put us on a small cliff above the sheep. We were within 250 yards, an easy shot for a rifleman, but impossible yardage for a bowhunter. I suggested that Rick and myself try to position ourselves around the cliff close to the sheep trail that ran along the base of the cliff. The others would circle around to the rams and walk down through the pass with the hope that the rams would veer away from them and blunder into me and Rick. Everyone liked the plan so Rick and I chose our spot and waited.

It happened fast. The rams suddenly materialized below us, with the biggest one in the lead. When he stopped, the other rams just plowed right into him, startling him for a second. Rick

There aren't many hunters who can say their first animal taken with a bow was a Rocky Mountain Bighorn sheep, but Paul Izanti can. His trophy scores 181⅝.

whispered for me to take him. I leaned forward and drew back the bow. I looked at the ram's horns and let the arrow fly. I heard the arrow hit, but couldn't see where.

The ram never ran, he just kept walking as did the rest of the band. I reached for a second arrow and took aim again. Rick told me to hold off. He said the ram was hit hard. The ram started weaving as it lead the rest of the herd into a clump of timber, then back out into the snow ahead of us. I felt helpless, I could see the arrow hanging from his neck but could do nothing but hope he would lay down.

One of the smaller rams must have sensed something was wrong because he suddenly bolted away from the lead ram and ran about 50 yards. When the big ram did not follow, the rest of the rams returned to the sheep trail and continued on as if they knew the old boy was dying. The ram laid down and rested his heavily horned head almost sleepily on the snow.

Rick and I literally leaped off the rocky cliff and ran to the ram. As we approached the ram we could just see how large and heavily broomed his horns really were. When Randy and John arrived, we spent several minutes reliving the excitement. When we hit Canamore a few hours later, we went to the best place in town for dinner. Later that night we measured the horns. While our numbers weren't official, they were close enough for us to realize that this ram would exceed the 180-point minimum for Boone & Crockett. After the 60-day drying period, the ram was officially scored at 181⅝ and made both Boone & Crockett and Pope & Young. My bighorn also won the gold award of excellence from Foundation of North American Wild Sheep for the largest ram taken with a bow.

This was truly a hunt to remember and I am really glad I chose to go with the bow. My ram holds a special place in my heart and my trophy room.

27

Big Bow & Arrow Bull

by Jerry Strodtman

I bugled and the bull answered. I bugled again. This time the bull screamed back and started moving towards us. I raised my bow and got ready.

My elk hunting adventures began two years ago when I talked my brother Roger into taking me bowhunting for elk in Montana. Roger is an avid rifle hunter and had been to Montana on four or five previous hunts, so he knew the area we were hunting well. I'm a dairy farmer in south-central Minnesota, so getting away in October to go rifle hunting is next to impossible with the harvest under way. I have hunted with a bow for nearly 20 years.

Prior to our first elk hunt in 1984, Roger and I attended Wayne Rogers' seminar on elk bugling. At the seminar we purchased his elk bugling tape, which gave step by step instructions for bugling sequences with a diaphragm call. I practiced my calling for the next three months.

Roger did most of the calling during the first hunt—when we finally located the elk. The first four or five days were a lesson in futility. We finally located a nice bull that Roger was able to call within 20 yards, but we never got a shot because we hadn't set up properly. The remainder of the hunt was terminated by a storm.

The following spring, when it came time to apply for our licenses, I couldn't talk Roger into hunting with a bow again. Roger had taken two bulls with his rifle so he wanted to hunt with a rifle again. I couldn't blame him.

My wife, Diane, decided that she would go with me. She didn't plan on hunting, but wanted to use the opportunity for a chance to take a much needed vacation. Living on a farm, we don't have many chances to take them.

To get in shape for the trip, Diane and I rode our bicycles four miles every morning after chores. I also practiced my bugling every chance I got. By the time of our hunt, we were both ready.

On September 13, we left our oldest son, Keith, in charge of the farm, and left for our destination in southwest Montana, about 60 miles northwest of Yellowstone National Park. When we arrived there late the next day, we set up our 10 x 12 tent, ate supper and hit the hay.

The next morning we got up early to find that someone had set up a tent in the middle of our hunting area, forcing us to hunt an area about 10 miles away. We walked up and down ridges all day but didn't see any elk. We did see two nice mule deer bucks, but didn't get close enough for a shot. We headed back to camp a little before dark to check out my preferred hunting spot and see who was camping there. As it turned out, it was a logger who had put his tent there for logging operations.

Early the next day we went up a logging trail as far as we could with our pickup. We were on Bureau of Land Management land so we were not allowed to use our vehicle beyond certain points. You can ride horses, or walk as we did. We scouted the ridges all day, finally finding a good-looking spot in a ravine.

I tried bugling there with the diaphragm call and grunt tube,

but got no answers. However, when we started to move on, we spooked two elk back up the mountain. Apparently they were coming to check us out. We stayed put and tried bugling again. This time I saw a 4x4 moving in front of me. He stopped about 75 yards away, just long enough for me to get a good look at him. To the right and behind him, I spotted some more movement, but couldn't positively identify the animals. We followed the animals for about a mile, but never got a good look at them. We finally headed back to camp.

The third day we decided to let the area cool down and hunted a different one about four miles southeast of there. We heard some elk bugling, but couldn't get any to respond to my calling.

The fourth day dawned cold, wet and miserable. I suggested to Diane that we sleep in, but she refused. I guess she actually liked stomping through the mountains. She said this was our day to get an elk. We headed back to the place we spotted the 4x4 two days before.

The elk were bugling up a storm on the mountain! We wanted to head straight up the mountain after them, but there was a strong breeze blowing right up the slope so we made a big circle to get around them. It sounded like four or five bulls were sounding off. I decided to bugle and got an answer immediately. The bull was across a ravine and below us. I called again and his answer indicated that he was moving toward us—that is until he got to the open ravine below us. I bugled several more times hoping to draw him across it, but he wouldn't budge. I told Diane ''We're going after him.''

Not caring about noise, Diane and I tore across the ravine and into the timber on the other side. We took cover in some brush and I bugled again. The bull screamed back and started coming toward us. We could hear him moving through the brush, but could not see him. Suddenly he appeared right in front of us! The trouble was, he came in so fast I wasn't able to get a shot. He spooked and ran back the way he came.

I immediately bugled again and grunted with my own voice. The bull turned around and started heading our way again, but stopped in some thick brush, offering no chance for a shot. Then another bull bugled nearby. This made the first bull very nervous and he ran back into the brush. Suddenly, the second elk came into view. I was shocked. It was a cow!

I got over the shock immediately when I spotted a huge 6x6 walk up behind her. He stopped 15 to 20 yards away in an opening

Jerry Strodtman's bowkilled elk scores 311⅛ Pope & Young points.

right in front of me. I brought my 70-pound Ben Pearson 4400 Magnum to full draw, put my 20-yard sight pin low in the bull's massive chest and released. The 2219 XX75 shaft tipped with a 3-bladed Rocky Mountain Supreme hit with a thud. The bull whirled and ran.

At that point, Diane and I were almost shaking with excitement. Diane asked how long we should wait and I figured about a half hour would be long enough. As it turned out, we waited only five minutes. It didn't matter, we found the bull piled up only 50 yards from where we stood.

Packing out the big bull took three trips and over twelve hours. We finally called it a day at about 10:30 that night, almost too tired to eat.

My bull scored 311⅛ Pope and Young points and was large enough to take first place in the Wapiti Division of the NAHC's 1985 Big Game Awards. Taking my bull was a thrill I'll never forget.

28

Yolla Bolly Blacktail

by Jay Gates

The Coast Range Mountains of northern California rise out of the Pacific Ocean, gradually sweep upward to over 6,000 feet, forming a barrier that separates the ocean from the inland valleys. Among these mountains are the oak and manzanita choked slopes, canyons and peaks of the Yolla Bolly Middle Eel Wilderness Area. Deep in this roadless tract, lies some of the finest Columbian blacktail habitat on the continent. It's the kind of place where trophy bucks reside, primarily because it's the kind of place few hunters ever wander into.

Jim Schaafsma, one of my oldest and best hunting companions, and one of the finest blacktail deer hunters in North America, has hunted this country for years. He used to guide there and knows the Trinity, Six Rivers, and Mendocino Forests better than anyone. Jim gave up his guide and outfitting business in 1984, so when I went to hunt with him in 1986, we were forced to hunt on public land because Jim no longer held trespass rights to some of the better private ranches.

After considerable deliberation, Jim decided we should go into the Yolla Bolly Wilderness which is about 60 miles west of Red Bluff and 80 miles in from the coast. Jim said that we would probably find more bucks up in the Salmon-Trinity Wilderness, but the bucks in the Yolla Bolly were of higher quality. The wilderness hunt suited me just fine since it meant we were going on my favorite kind of hunt—a long backpack hunt.

We had six days to spend in the wilderness looking for trophy bucks. We left the Eureka Airport and headed east and south to a jumping off place east of the Middle Eel River, which would, with a few hours of walking, put us well away from civilization and into blacktail country.

Shouldering our packs, we made use of Forest Service trails for a while before jumping off to bushwack through and over a series of big canyons and rocky ridges. The manzanita brush was so thick that there were times when it clutched at my feet and legs like red-skinned monsters in a nightmare. Our campsite was ideal, next to a nice running stream, but the first three days of the hunt proved fruitless. Part of the problem was the weather. It was excessively hot, as only the late Indian Summer days can be in this part of the country. We prayed for bad weather.

For the second half of the hunt we drove to the south end of the wilderness area. From the road we followed game trails which led us deeper into the wilderness and into more good habitat. After setting up camp, we made a brief scout of the region, but the sign of trophy animals was discouragingly lacking.

Early the next day, we headed even deeper into the Yolla Bolly, finally finding sign of blacktail. Encouraged, we kicked canyons and walked the ridges. It was hot and getting hotter, making any activity difficult. Even glassing was tough because of the heat waves. But we knew that if we were going to find a trophy buck under these conditions, we would have to cover a lot of ground, so we just kept working. Just after midday, the work finally paid off.

I spotted a nice buck grazing with three does and a smaller male. Careful scrutiny through the Bushnell spotting scope confirmed that this was indeed a prize blacktail. I told Jim that it was the buck I wanted.

After a brief stalk, I got into position with the buck 150 yards away on a sidehill. It was a clean, broadside shot. I steadied the Remington Model 700 .270 Winchester on a rock, put the crosshairs of the scope on the target and squeezed off a single round. As the echo of the report bounced around the hills of the Yolla Bolly, the buck turned and ran straight downhill and out of sight. For a split second I thought I had missed, but when we rushed to the spot where the buck was standing when I fired there was blood sprayed on the ground. We found my trophy 125 yards later.

If it lives in North America, walks on four hooves and goes by the name of deer, Jay Gates can find trophy specimens. Proof is in animals like this Yolla Bolly blacktail that scores 140 net.

He was a "buster buck." Jim felt even better about him than I did. I made a field appraisal of 130-135 points, Jim thought he was better, and he was—144 points gross and 140 net. We caped the head and boned the carcass before packing the animal back to camp. We made camp just at nightfall.

The next day we went looking for Jim's buck. Again at midday, we spotted a nice buck on a ridge 200 yards away. We moved into position for a better look. I asked Jim what he thought. He gave a low whistle indicating he liked what he saw.

"But I don't think I want him," he said.

I asked him if he had taken leave of his senses. "He'll go 145 gross," I said.

"Nah, I don't want him," he said, but then I saw the twinkle in Schaafsma's eye — it's the one he gets when he's jerking your chain.

"Gotcha, Gates," he laughed.

"You still have to hit him," I chided.

Jim answered with a single shot that brought the buck down. Jim's trophy measured slightly less than mine did (143 gross, 138 net); his twelfth Boone and Crockett blacktail. After the caping and boning, we packed the prize back to camp.

The incredible success of the hunt had temporarily put out of mind the fact that we still had more than six hours of hard packing between us and the truck. And now, besides the packs we had brought in, we had two heavy bucks to take out. It would require every minute of light and a lot of hard work in the next days just to get everything to the road.

At first light, we each hefted a carcass and headed south. We stopped at what we guessed to be two hours from the truck. While Jim went on with one buck, I went back to get the camp. By the time I finally returned, it was close to dark and Jim had managed to get both bucks to the vehicle.

Jim and I had been walking and packing for nearly 11 hours that final day. We killed our bucks in very rugged country, more than 4 miles from camp and 8 to 10 from the road. In country like the Yolla Bolly, it sometimes take an hour to cover one mile.

I get a special feeling from leaving behind the vehicle that has become a way of life for most people and heading off into the woods or mountains to meet my quarry on his own terms. To me it's part of what hunting is all about.

29

1,600 Pound Brown Bear

by Lawrence Sheets

A sudden movement on the hillside above us caught our attention. It was the bear, and he was only 100 yards away. I quickly searched for some kind of rest, but there was nothing in sight. I had to take the brownie with an offhand shot.

Back in May of 1982, two friends, Lester Carr, Jr., Conda Shanholtz and I left for a bear hunt with Outfitter Gene Needles of Chugiak, Alaska. It was a successful hunt for the whole party and especially for me. I received the 1982 Firearms Award from the North Amercian Hunting Club for taking the biggest brown bear that year.

We left our homes in West Virginia and flew to Seattle, Washington, where we caught another flight to Anchorage. We stayed in Gene's home that night. In the morning, we boarded a Cessna 185 and flew to his base camp on the Martins River in the Copper River Drainage east of Cordova.

The snow was still three and a half feet deep when we arrived, but it was melting fast. It had been up to the eaves of the camp roof just a week earlier when Gene and his guides, Jim and Sam Fejes, came in to set everything up.

We stayed in main camp that night and in the morning flew out to spike camps. My guide, Sam, and I set up camp near the base of a large glacier. The next morning, we spotted a large black bear on a hillside above us. We put on our snowshoes and hustled after him. Two miles later we relocated him after a brief search. The bear winded us as I set up to shoot, but I dropped the hammer as he turned to leave. The bear rolled part way down the hill and landed behind some brush. We skinned him out and headed back to camp. It was rather late when we finally made it back, but Sam wanted to return to the base camp because we hadn't spotted any brown bear. I agreed. A hot meal and shower would feel good after a long day.

Conda came back to camp late in the afternoon of the fourth day. He had taken a nice brownie earlier that morning after it almost walked into camp. The pilot told me to get my gear ready as soon as possible because Conda's guide, Jim, was waiting for me back at the camp. Jim thought they had a wounded bear in the area and wanted me to help him track it down and kill it. We loaded my gear and flew to camp.

I spotted the bear's tracks as we were landing. They lead from the river to some alder bushes a short distance from camp. It was almost dark by the time we had unloaded the plane and had my gear stowed away, but we tried to follow the tracks anyway. I didn't relish the thought of having a wounded bear so close to camp.

Darkness overtook us before we made the willows, forcing us to return to camp. I spent a very nervous night. I kept my loaded rifle next to my bed in case the bear came into camp.

We got up early the next morning and struck out in search of the bear. We followed the creek banks because the snow was still over three feet deep in the brush. We walked about three miles up the Martins River, but saw no sign of the wounded bear. We spotted another large bear on a snow slide along the base of a mountain about a mile away.

The wind was right, so we decided to wait awhile and see what the bear would do. It was possible that he would decide to head toward the river, saving us a tough walk. Two and a half hours later he came off the snow slide and started feeding on some willow buds. Jim decided it was time to take a closer look.

We closed the range to 350 yards and stopped behind an old log to wait awhile longer. The bear started feeding away from us, so we left our packs and equipment behind and moved closer. There wasn't much cover so we had to be careful, moving only when the bear put his head down to feed. We kept moving for what seemed like hours. Jim wanted to get as close as possible.

We were probably 80 yards from the bear when he fed behind some brush and disappeared. He reappeared a few minutes later

about 100 yards from us. I quickly looked for a rest, but couldn't find anything. I finally decided to shoot offhand.

When my .300 Weatherby Magnum cracked, the bear lost his footing and started sliding down the hill toward us. He was still struggling when he made it to the bottom, so I shot again, not wanting him to get back on his feet. He stayed down.

I knew the bear was big before I shot, but I didn't realize how big he really was. His front feet were 10½ inches wide, 12 inches from toe to heel. His back feet were 15½ inches long and his head measured 21 inches from his ear to the end of his nose. Jim told me he would probably square 10 feet, which later proved to be an underestimation. He actually squared 11 feet. Both the guide and the outfitter agreed that he weighed between 1,600 and 1,800 pounds!

It took us four hours to skin the bear and load it on Jim's

packboard. He started for camp, leaving me to pack the rest of the gear. It was almost dark by the time we made it back to our tent. I slept well that night.

Early the next morning we put out the signal for the plane to land. It arrived about noon. There was a great celebration in camp that evening after Lester returned with a nice 8½-foot brown bear and a large black bear. All three of us had scored on nice bears, both brownies and blacks. Not bad for a 10-day hunt.

Gene Needles has guided bear hunters for many years. During that time, he has been in on the kills of more than 2,200 bears. He said my bear topped them all. Gene and Jim measured the bear skull after it was skinned. It measured 28¹⁄₁₆ green. I had both my bears mounted life-size. The brown bear stands 9½ feet tall and the black bear a little over seven feet.

30

Wyoming Whitetail
The Hard Way

by Dale Critchfield

My hunt began in late October of 1984 and didn't end until I pulled the trigger on October 26th, 1986. The hunt was a lesson in patience and perseverance, which I consider two of the most important ingredients of a successful hunt.

In October of 1984, an acquaintance and myself were hunting antelope west of Cheyenne without any luck. Having thoroughly hunted the area and with darkness approaching, we decided to call it a day. On the way out of the hunting area we had to drive parallel to a small creek. The setting sun was shining into our eyes as we were driving, but we still managed to see an animal's silhouette against the evening sky. My hunting companion thought it was an antelope, but I could tell by its shape that it was a deer. I glassed the buck with my small Pentax binoculars and I was surprised to see that it was a premium whitetail buck. I knew there were whitetails in the creekbed, but I never thought much about hunting the area.

Several years earlier, I had taken a nice four point whitetail buck (western count) in this area that I had mounted. Since I already had one whitetail on the wall, I didn't try too hard to bag another. The sight of this buck piqued my interest.

I knew that the owner of this ranch hadn't allowed anyone to hunt deer for about eight years. I realized that it would be difficult to obtain permission, but I felt that the work would be justified by having the chance to bag such a whitetail. I immediately started to work on a plan to gain this rancher's confidence and possibly his friendship. I began stopping by his house periodically for a little small talk, sometimes bringing a small gift to show my appreciation for the hunts I had previously taken on his land. During one visit in the spring he stated that he had some beavers that were causing problems in a couple of his irrigation ditches. I hadn't trapped for several years, but I volunteered to trap the problem animals. I borrowed some traps from a friend and in the next few days managed to alleviate his problem. During my spare time, I dug the canal a little wider because it had silted in where the beavers had made dams. I notified the rancher that I thought I had the problem solved and told him I would call him in a few days to see if I was correct. When I called him back, he said the water was running better than ever and that he was very grateful. He said that if there was ever anything he could help me with to just say so. I felt that now was as good a time as any to ask his permission to hunt on his land. I popped the question, letting him know that I was willing to obey any restrictions he placed on my hunting the area. He said that would be fine with him and just asked that I try to avoid shooting in the vicinity of his cattle. His saying "yes" affirmed my strong belief that a true hunter will sometimes spend more time "hunting" a place to hunt then actually hunting. Thousands of prime hunting spots are being overlooked or avoided by hunters because they have to get landowners' permission or do a little research work in finding out the status of the land.

When it came time to submit applications for the 1985 big game permits, I applied for the limited quota deer area in which the ranch was located. I eagerly awaited the drawing results which would be available in about a month. I had approximately an 85 percent chance of drawing this area so I felt confident of my chances. The day of the drawing came and to my surprise, I did not draw a deer license in this area! This was strictly a limited area and therefore I would not be able to hunt there during the 1985 season. This was a big disappointment, but I do concur with the Game & Fish Department's theory that some of the hunting areas in the state have to be hunted on a limited basis to properly manage the herds.

For the next year and a half I watched the whitetails in my hunting area. I spotted several real nice whitetail bucks during scouting trips and felt that when I could obtain a license that my chances of success were excellent. I was reserving a spot on my wall for another whitetail buck.

Dale Critchfield's Wyoming whitetail trophy represents not only hunting success, but a real appreciation of the landowner/hunter relationship.

I was very anxious to see what type of seasons the Game and Fish Department would have in this area for fall of 1986. I was elated to find out that they had allocated some extra licenses for whitetails that would go on sale in July on a first-come, first-serve basis. I obtained the proper applications and made sure that my application was submitted as early as possible. I finally had a license to pursue one of those whitetail bucks!

I was unable to hunt the opening week of the season because I was very busy, but I was able to get out the second. The hunt was more difficult than I thought it would be. What made it so difficult to get close enough for a shot was the open, flat prairie land surrounding the small creek. I tried two separate stalks on one particular buck over the next several days, but was unsuccessful both times. My opportunity came on my third attempt. I spotted a small herd of whitetails with a couple good bucks in a small meadow along a cliff. I had to get on my hands and knees and crawl about 100 yards during the final stages of the stalk, but when I peered over the edge of the cliff I knew I had them. They were feeding only 100 yards away.

There were two bucks in the herd, one a 4x4, the other a 3x3. I took a moment to take a close look at both of them, finally deciding to shoot the 3x3 because his antlers were larger, thicker and would be more attractive on my wall. I lined up my Remington Model 788 .243 Winchester with a Harris Ultralight bipod attached. I have taken about 40 head of big game with this rifle, so I have complete confidence in it. I waited until the buck turned broadside, placed the crosshairs behind the front shoulder and squeezed the trigger.

The report of my rifle was still echoing in my ears when the sound of the bullet finding its target reached me. The buck ran about 30 yards into a small weedpatch and fell. I lay there a moment to make sure that as I walked the buck wouldn't get up and run, forcing me to take a running shot. My anxiety got the best of me and I headed for the buck. He was dead when I found him. It was a satisfying moment to finally obtain a trophy buck that I had watched for almost two years.

The most satisfying part of this hunt was all the work and preparation that went into it. I believe that all of us hunters should remember what I call the four P's — patience, perseverance, permission, and placement (bullet). I know that these will be some of the foremost thoughts in my mind as I pursue the much larger five pointer I have spotted this season!

31

The Ice-Breaker

by Troy Graziadei

"There, on the ridgeline! Caribou!! Bulls!!! Big bulls!!!" After suffering through three days of terrible weather, complete with rain, snow and very few caribou, my voice didn't hide the excitement I felt. I looked over at my partners John Dodge and Todd Smith and could tell they felt the same way.

Hunting caribou on the open tundra is pretty tough, especially with a bow and arrow. Nothing grows very tall out here and we were probably 50 miles from the nearest tree. This made stalking very difficult. The only thing I could hope for was to locate caribou near some type of knoll, rock-cropping or bluff to offer some sort of cover.

All of us live in Fairbanks, Alaska, where John owns Bighorn Archery, a small shop which specializes in traditional archery equipment. John had custom-built beautiful longbows for Todd and me a few months prior to our hunt. He also outfitted us with a matched set of Port Orford cedar arrows. I have to admit, I've never known anyone to put more time and craftsmanship into their work than John. I personally feel he is unsurpassed as a bowyer and arrow maker.

After getting our longbows, Todd and I desperately wanted to take them out hunting. I had always shot a compound bow and Todd a recurve, so this was a first for both of us using a "stick bow." For several weeks we practiced steadily on paper targets and small game, both getting quite proficient with our new equipment. We decided these were the bows we would use during the upcoming hunting season. We got together with John and after much talk our hunt was planned. We would hunt caribou above the Arctic Circle in August. Todd and I had never taken any big game with a bow before, even though we have hunted several years. John, who is an older fellow with much experience and success with a bow, was really looking forward to seeing Todd and me possibly score our first big game on a trip with him.

I sure hoped I could break the ice. Bowhunters say once you get that first one under your belt, others come more frequently. I must say, though, that I have always felt that the hunt itself is the most important—not the game taken. The game taken is a bonus. It's the hunt itself from which I gain the most enjoyment. That is why year after year I keep taking my bow even though I've been unsuccessful.

We had left Fairbanks the second week of August and drove north on some 400 miles of gravel road to get there. I'm sure it was the roughest road in North America, as we all felt we were in a popcorn popper the whole trip. In spite of the bad road, we had driven through some of the most beautiful country in the world, going right through the heart of the majestic Brooks Range. It was amazing to think that we had set up camp only 100 miles or so from the Arctic Ocean.

The big bulls I had spotted on the distant ridge turned out to be four magnificent bulls, all having massive antlers covered with dark velvet. It was still too early for them to start rubbing their velvet, which they usually do in late August or early September. We were sure all four were trophy class, as their bodies looked out of proportion carrying those large antlers. The ridgeline was broken up by a small draw in which a narrow stream of water flowed. We could see that the stream had some brush growing along its edges, which would offer some type of cover. We decided this would be the best route for a stalk. Three of the bulls were bedded on the left side of the draw, the other bull on the right. I was sure they were up there letting the wind help keep the bugs off of them. The sun had come out, making it very warm. The bugs were quite thick, also making it quite uncomfortable for us.

John and Todd let me know it was my turn for a stalk and that I'd better get going before those bulls decided to leave the country. We had all agreed that on each stalk, one of us was enough. It was just too difficult for two or three of us to get within bow range

A bull caribou is a magnificent trophy for any hunter, but to make one your first big game animal with a longbow is an accomplishment few hunters achieve today.

without spooking the game, especially on the open tundra.

I grabbed my quiver of arrows and my bow, then headed across the tundra for the small stream that drained the ridge. When I reached the stream, I decided my best bet was to stay low and follow it, since it did offer some waist-high brush for cover. As I crept along, I kept the bulls in sight the whole time. After about an hour of this, I had managed to get within 150 yards without alarming them. I had found a nice clump of bushes in which I could conceal myself while I watched and waited for the caribou to do something. I knew I just couldn't go out on the open ridge without spooking them. I got my knife out and cut small branches, which I placed in my hat for camouflage, figuring I would need all the help I could get. I looked up to check the caribou. To my surprise, the lone bull on the right had gotten up and started feeding. He was slowly working his way toward the head of the draw, probably to cross over and join the others.

I knew I couldn't waste any time. I had to estimate where he would cross and hopefully I could get there in time to intercept him. I slowly eased my way up the draw, staying very low and using the brush for cover. About 50 yards into the stalk, the narrow draw turned into a good-sized gully. I couldn't believe it! How lucky could I get? I dropped down into the gully and stayed completely out of sight, hiding behind its banks. I was able to move much more quickly now and soon I was at the spot I figured he would cross. I took a few seconds to catch my breath, then eased up over the bank just enough to see if I could locate him. My head went quickly back down — the bull was only 25 yards away feeding broadside!

I could feel my heart pounding like a drum as I quietly nocked an arrow. I told myself to stay calm and pick a spot, just don't shoot at the whole animal. I gently raised up, the bull was still in the same place and unaware of my presence. I slowly drew my bow back, concentrating on a small white patch behind his front shoulder. After a smooth release, I could tell my arrow flew straight and true as it hit its mark. The bull flinched and then staggered off some 30 yards before falling. I stood there gazing at my downed bull, as I knew I had taken my first big game with a bow.

I looked back to where John and Todd had been watching and they had already started up the slope toward me. When they arrived, there were many handshakes as they told me how much they enjoyed watching the entire stalk. We took lots of pictures, then began skinning the bull.

The hunt turned out to be very enjoyable and successful for all of us. John and Todd also scored on nice caribou, making it three out of three. My bull ended up scoring 325⅜, enough to make the Pope and Young record book.

I'll look back on this hunt for a lifetime, as it was the hunt I had finally broken that ever so thick ice.

32

Muskox At
78 Degrees Below Zero
by John McAteer

My trip actually started in August of 1985, when I saw a special documentary on Arctic Tundra Life. It was then that I contemplated hunting muskox in their harsh climate. I contacted the North American Hunting Club and got all of the pertinent information on outfitters located in the Northwest Territories. I made my selection and decided to go with Klineburger World Wide Travel and Guided Arctic Expeditions. My equipment selection would have to be critical because of the temperatures in which I would be hunting, and the type of game I had selected. My quarry was one of the most misunderstood creatures God ever created—the muskox. This walking carpet has been covering the Arctic and parts of Alaska from the dawn of time and is one of the only animals on the face of the earth that still looks like it came from prehistoric times.

I arrived in Invik Northwest Territories during the month of March and caught a shuttle flight from there to Banks Island, my final destination. I was amazed at how cold it was there. When I left New York, it was 50 degrees Fahrenheit. When I stepped off the plane on Banks Island it was 20 degrees below zero. On my arrival, I was greeted by my two Eskimo guides named Roy Goose and Pat Kudluck. With me on this trip was my good friend and cameraman, Thomas Berry. By the end of this trip, both Tom and I would learn a great deal from our two northern friends about survival in the vast Arctic Tundra.

The four of us started across the north Arctic ice on sleds with outside temperatures about 25 degrees below zero. The cold, although dry, was as sharp as a knife on our skin. We traveled about fifty miles the first day and set up our spike camp on an unnamed frozen tundra lake. The second morning, it was about 35 degrees below zero, and temperatures were dropping! I was the first of our group to experience frostbite on my face. With the help of a good face mask and my ability to heal fast, I was back to normal on the fourth day.We started to see small herds of muskox and caribou. I was amazed at the animal's speed and endurance.

The fifth day brought us deeper into the Arctic with colder temperatures. We started to see larger herds of muskox and traces of wolves. I spotted a very majestic muskox alone near a large glacier formation. I took off after him alone, which proved almost a fatal mistake. I never should have separated from the group. I confronted him at the bottom of a fiord and turned to see if the rest of my group was behind me. The muskox charged, knocking both me and my snowmobile over. It took me a couple of minutes to collect my thoughts before I righted my machine and went to find the rest of my group. They found me. My guide said I was lucky that we didn't have a white out, which is very common during that time of year. He said we should stay together. I agreed with a great sigh.

I went back after the bull. He had traveled far from where I first cornered him. I caught up to him about three miles later. Roy Goose directed me to stalk the bull from above. I took my bow from the case and started on foot across a frozen lake until I was about 200 yards above him. He was feeding across the plush Arctic tundra. As I approached him, I was very apprehensive after the incident on the snowmobile. I stalked him, keeping large snow drifts between him and me. When I finally stalked within about 35 yards, I decided to take the shot. But when I tried to remove an arrow from the quiver, I found that they were all frozen into the rubber guides. The temperature was about 50 degrees below zero with a 20 mile an hour wind, making the windchill 78 degrees below zero. I cut the arrow from the quiver with my knife and drew back my bow, not knowing what to expect with the temperature so cold. As I released the arrow, I prayed that the bow would not fail me.

The arrow connected, but it was a little low. The muskox reared and took off across the flats of ice before coming to a halt

In temperatures that dropped to 78 degrees below zero, John McAteer took this bull that ranks as the Number Seven bowkill ever.

about 200 yards in front of me. I pursued him. He knew that I was coming, but he held his ground. I had lost the feeling in my left hand and was afraid I was not going to be able to take a second shot. I stalked him again, this time getting within 20 yards. My second shot hit the mark and I was glad because there was no feeling in either of my hands by that time. The bull ran about 50 yards and dropped.

My muskox has given me new feelings about hunting the Arctic. I felt we were both evenly matched. I respect both the animal I harvested and the beauty that will draw me back whether it be in mind or on any other adventure.

Later, my bull scored 107⅘ Pope & Young points, only four points shy of the world record and good enough for seventh place. Fellow NAHC member Theodore Dzienir holds sixth place with a bull that scores 108 even.

If you would like to take record-class muskox, head for Banks Island, Northwest Territories. Five of the top eight trophies were taken there. One of them is mine.

33

Boone & Crockett Black Bear

by Sam Harrelson

Early in March I decided to add a bear rug to my collection of game animals. Having hunted bear only once before, and that was in Idaho with a bow, I started talking to people in the area on the do's and don'ts of hunting them in Colorado. Every story I got was different, so I decided to use a local newspaper story as a guide. In that story, the bears were baited so I set out collecting jack rabbits, meat scraps, old bread and anything else I could think of that would rot and smell.

A few weeks later, on April 8 to be exact, my wife gave me some friendly advice—either clean the garage out or she would. I figured my bait was ripe enough, so I loaded it into my 4x4 and headed to an area near the Eleven Mile Reservoir. This area was chosen after talking to friends who had seen bears in the area every spring.

Two hours later I arrived at the area, with my Pike National Forest Bait permit and the bait. The bait was placed, the permit hung from a tree in a jelly jar, and the waiting began. I had decided to check the bait on Wednesdays and weekends until the bears had come to the bait. I checked the bait on April 11—no bears. I checked it again on April 14—no bears but lots of snow. I started to wonder what I was doing wrong. I decided to add some fish to the bait; you always see bears eating fish in the outdoors, right?

I got about 50 pounds of suckers and let them ripen for a week or so and placed them at the bait station on May 9. On May 12, the bait was checked and every last crumb was gone. My plans changed, I would use nothing but fish. Then problems beset me.

I had to work long hours the next week and a half and didn't have time to get bait and drive up at night to restock the site. After the flap at work was over, I decided to take some vacation time and spend four or five solid days over the bait. On May 22, I got 100 pounds of suckers and rebaited. I returned on Monday, May 24, and promptly buried my 4x4 to the rear axle in mud. I decided to leave the truck alone—it wasn't going anywhere—and start hunting.

I selected a stand along a hillside about 125 yards from the bait and got settled. It started to rain and snow, but I was determined to stick it out. Fifteen hours later I headed back to my truck, soaked and disgusted. I hadn't seen a thing.

The next day, I was back on the stand at daylight with some cold sandwiches and a Pepsi. It rained or snowed all morning but cleared up as the day went on. About 2:30 p.m., a fair size sow came to the bait. I decided she was good enough and squeezed off a round. She whirled around and ran into the deep timber. I waited 30 minutes and carefully followed. No tracks could be found as the aspen leaves were six to eight inches deep. I moved in the general area she had gone.

About 75-100 yards from the bait I saw her moving through the rocks above me. I waited for another clear shot and squeezed it off carefully. She disappeared. I wasn't sure if she was dead so I circled around and above her. When I got up to the spot she was standing, she wasn't there. I became a little jittery. "I couldn't have missed," I thought to myself. "Not at 30 yards." Circling the area she was last seen didn't help. No bear.

Three hours later, help came up the road. I ran to my truck and told my story to three rescuers. They offered to help. We searched the area until dark, but found only one small drop of blood high on the ridge some three to four hundred yards from where she was last seen. We decided that I had just nicked her. She wasn't hurt badly and would survive. No further attempt was made to find her. However, I glassed the area the next day and kept an eye out for her when on stand.

I was back on my stand at daylight, with more sandwiches and Pepsi. Finally, about 3:30 p.m., a huge bear approached the bait through the trees. He wouldn't come into the bait, appearing very cautious, and eased out of the area. Then he moved into the edge of

the clearing where I could shoot. I laid my rifle on a rest and squeezed at his neck. The "Big One" just whirled into the trees and disappeared.

I tracked this one for hours and hours without spotting even one drop of blood. A complete miss! I started questioning myself, questioning my gun, questioning everything. No answers. It was back to the truck where I laid awake most of the night wondering what went wrong.

I awoke Thursday with renewed interest and sunshine in my face. It was the last day I could spend hunting as my daughter was graduating from Coronado High School the next morning. The hunt was a bust. I returned to my truck at dark after a whole day of seeing nothing. I decided to check my rifle while home to make sure it was okay. To my surprise, it was shooting eight inches low at 100 yards. That sure answered some of my questions. I had just committed the biggest hunting sin. I had never checked my rifle to see if it was shooting straight. That will never happen again. While there, I sighted in my new .300 Winchester Magnum and decided to use it on my next trip.

After my daughter's graduation and my 20th wedding anniversary celebration, it was time for more vacation and hunting. New bait and interest, a good rifle and I was back on the stand. I didn't see anything the first two days, so it was with some difficulty that I dragged myself out of bed at 5:00 a.m. and back on my stand.

By noon, I had decided that I had blown the two chances I was going to get and probably wasn't going to get another. As the day went along I became more and more discouraged, finally deciding to leave for home at dark. I looked at my watch. It was 5:30 p.m. "I'll stay until 6:00," I told myself. When 6:00 arrived, I decided to stick it out until 7:00. When 7:00 arrived, I talked myself into staying until the end of the day, which meant 8:51, one half hour after sunset. At 8:30 p.m. I started getting everything ready to leave. Pockets full, I took one more look at the bait. My heart almost stopped. A giant bear was in the middle of the clearing and heading toward the bait!

I quickly grabbed my binoculars to get a good look at him. They confirmed my first impression. I continued watching him until he neared the bait, then put my glasses down and picked up my rifle. My heart was pounding. I was shaking all over. I couldn't hold it still. "Lay the gun down," I told myself. "Now relax. This is no different than a big elk!" "Who are you trying to kid?" the other side of me answered moments before I got my emotions under control. I finally picked up my rifle, aimed carefully and squeezed the trigger.

The bear dropped immediately, but started flailing and pawing at the ground in an attempt to get up. Unable to do so, he opened his mouth, rolled back his lips and gave several loud snarls and roars. He died as his last roar echoed throughout the surrounding canyons.

He was certainly a mean looking old fellow. I was glad to be 100 yards away. Then it dawned on me, I had my bear! I looked at my watch, it read 8:40, just 11 minutes before the end of legal shooting time. I eased down to the bear to make sure it was dead. Loaded rifle in my left hand, a long aspen branch in the right, I approached ever so carefully and poked him a few times here and there. I was satisfied he was dead. I dropped all my gear and headed back to the truck.

I couldn't get my headlights pointed at the right angle to help while I field dressed the animal. I finally took my lantern out of the back of my truck. Have you ever tried to field dress an animal while holding a knife in one hand and a lantern in the other? It doesn't work. I finally gave up trying and did the job by feel alone. After several inspections by lamp, I decided it would have to do until I could get him home. Then it struck me. How was I going to get this big guy in my truck, especially since I couldn't even budge him.

It was time for a smoke anyway, so I sat on the tailgate and thought about it. "Here's the problem," I said to myself. "You have one big bear that has to go into the truck. The tools you have include two knives, a big game hoist, one large rope, a long chain and a pack board to do it."

Finishing my smoke, I decided to wrap the chain around a tree, hook the game hoist to the bear and lift him up and into the truck. Easy, right? Wrong! My first attempt failed because the chain wasn't high enough. On my second attempt, the rope jumped the track and jammed between the housing and pulley. I went back up the tree, unhooked everything, dug the rope out with a screw driver, hooked everything back up and started pulling again. This time, everything was working as planned, and I was able to back the truck under him. He was finally in!

The impossible completed, I headed home where two of my friends helped me skin and quarter him. At 4:00 a.m., I headed for the sack. It wasn't until the next morning, when I took the skin to

Sam Harrelson poses with the life-size mount of his Boone & Crockett black bear.

the taxidermist, that I really found out how big he was. His live weight was estimated at 400 pounds. Dave Martin, of Timberline Taxidermy told me, "You ought to have him checked for the record book because I will have to use an extra large grizzly bear head form to mount him."

The bear measured green 13 inches in length and 8⁵⁄₁₆ inches in width for a total of 21⁹⁄₁₆ inches, well above Boone & Crockett's minimum of 21. When the 60-day drying period ended, my bear officially scored 21¹⁄₁₆, good enough for a tie for 21st place in Boone & Crockett's 18th scoring period. I was thrilled!

34

**President's
Trophy Winner**

Caribou of a Lifetime

by Lawrence Alma

The stalk was going well. Ron and I had already narrowed the distance to 60 yards. But we had to get closer. The thick brush surrounding the bull hid everything but his antlers. I couldn't shoot even if I wanted to.

I am strictly a bowhunter. I have been bowhunting for 15 years. I am a Life Member of the NAHC, the NRA and the Colorado Bowhunters Association, where I served on the Board of Directors for five years. I am also a member of the Pope & Young Bowhunters of Wyoming.

During most of the off-season I shoot about 100 arrows per week, but beginning two months before the season, I shoot 100 arrows a day at ranges from 10 to 40 yards. I use no sights or arrow rest other than the shelf on the bow. My bow is a 67-pound Bighorn recurve with a Bighorn quiver. I make my own arrows using Easton Gamegetter 2020 aluminum shafts with Black Diamond Delta Broadheads.

That is the background I took into my 1984 hunt with Love Brothers & Lee in British Columbia. I had hunted with them before, but this time it was special because I was participating in one of the NAHC's Life Member Hunts.

I arrived in Smithers, British Columbia the day before the hunt and picked up my moose, caribou and goat licenses. My first preference was a goat. I had taken a nanny in 1982 that scored 43

P&Y points and I wanted to get a good billy to go with her.

I flew into camp the next morning, and by early afternoon we were hunting moose at the other end of the lake. The next day, we moved to another lake where we were to hike into a spike camp and hunt goats. My guide, Ron Fleming, and I hiked about four hours down to the Duti River. We stripped down to our underwear to wade the river. About halfway across, I thought my legs were going to give out. The water was so cold it numbed them.

After reaching the bank, we moved downstream to our camp site. In camp, Ron started a fire to fix a pot of coffee. I went to check out the area, but when I looked down the river valley I saw a storm moving in. Ron and I agreed that if we were going to get a camp set up without getting wet, we had better get with it. By the time the tent was up, the rain had hit. It rained all night and into the morning. The fog was right down on the tree tops. Goat hunting was out of the question.

We broke camp and headed back out. It took us eight hours to hike up out of there and it rained all the way. We stayed in a cabin on the lake for the night. With gear and spirits equally dampened, we flew out the next morning to another camp to hunt moose until the weather broke.

That afternoon, we headed down the Firesteel River looking for moose. Late that day I spotted a big caribou above timberline across the river. I pointed him out to Ron and he said we'd go up there first thing in the morning. That bull sure rekindled those dampened spirits.

The next morning, I could hardly wait to get going. It was a three-hour hike to timberline. We came out of the timber just below and to the right of the bowl in which we expected to find the caribou. We checked the wind, and it was wrong for us to go into the bowl from where we were. Ron suggested that we circle the bowl and enter it from the backside.

It was after noon by the time we reached that back rim and started glassing the bowl. I stepped up to the edge of the rim and right below me on a snow pack lay a small caribou bull. We looked closer and spotted five other caribou—all cows and calves. A short time later, Ron spotted a nice bull crossing the bowl, but it apparently had places to go. It didn't even slow down.

After we lost sight of it, I began telling Ron about a couple of small bull caribou that Bill Love and I had put a stalk on during my 1982 visit. As I was pointing out the path we took on the stalk up a small creek, I spotted a big bull standing in the middle of the

A NAHC Life Member hunt with Love Bros. & Lee produced this record book mountain caribou bull for Larry Alma.

creek bed. Needless to say, the storytelling ended quickly.

Ron said that we would have to go over the edge of the bowl right where we were because the way the flies were bothering them, the animals would not stay in one place very long. It was the best plan for a stalk, but in front of us was a rock slide that ran 250 yards to the bottom of the bowl. I kept watching the small bull, thinking he would spot us and ruin our plans, but he was more interested in avoiding the flies than anything else.

We somehow made it past him and the five other caribou and got to the bottom of the slide. We started across, constantly watching the big bull. He had moved out of the creek and laid down in a small patch of ground balsam.

That forced us to change our plans. We were going to follow

the creek bottom after crossing the slide, but I thought the way the bull was laying he would spot us. I suggested we circle around to our right and cross the creek right in front of him. That was the direction we took.

Still keeping a cautious eye on the other caribou, we slowly made our way to a knoll directly across the creek from where the caribou was laying.

I told Ron I was going to take my boots off to finish the stalk, because walking in boots was making too much noise. Ron did, too.

The rest of the knoll was only 60 yards from where the bull was bedded. We started over the knoll, watching the bull all the way. All I could see was his antlers. Suddenly, he turned his head. I froze, wondering if he had seen me. He hadn't. I stayed motionless until he turned his head back, then continued to move down and across the creek. We were now 30 yards from the bull. Ron stopped and whispered, "Go ahead."

That's when I really started to feel the excitement. It would have been easy to rush things at that point, but there was only one way to get the shot I wanted; to move s-l-o-w-l-y. I eased into action, heading toward a small opening to my right. Foot by foot the distance closed. I was now 20 yards from the bull. The brush was still too thick. I moved even closer. Fifteen yards now, and I still didn't have a clear shot. With my heart pounding I closed the distance to 10 yards. Finally! I drew and released.

The bull boiled out of his bed and raced up the creek about 50 yards before turning around and coming back down. He passed us like a freight train, his hooves churning up stones and sticks. I was so excited I followed him in my stocking feet. I ran over 100 yards of rocks to a vantage point where I could watch him. He went about 400 yards and stopped.

Ron and I put our boots back on and sat down to eat a candy bar. When I finally calmed down, we went after the bull. He was still alive when we got to him, so I finished him with a final arrow.

My hunt ended without me getting the goat I was after, but I couldn't have asked for a better hunt. All in all it was fantastic! Anyway, who could possibly complain after arrowing a 335-point plus Pope & Young caribou? Not me—that's for sure!

35

Archery Whitetail

by Ralph Herron

As the doe drew nearer, I spotted another movement in the tamaracks behind her. It was a buck, and holy cow what a buck! I raised my bow and prepared myself for the shot.

The 1984 Kansas bowhunting season is now history, but for this bowhunter, it will always be remembered as *the* season of my hunting career. For that year, I had the good fortune of bagging my first Pope & Young buck, a 12-point whitetail with an official score of 164⅞.

Like a large percentage of bowhunters, I started hunting deer with a rifle. In 1969, I killed my first deer with a Springfield .30-06. I remember thinking at the time, what a big thrill that it was. Three more followed in 1972, 1975, and 1978 all with a rifle.

Several factors led me to bowhunting. For one thing, the rifle hunting seasons were just too darned short. I had been a hunter most all of my life, and I love to hunt just for hunting's sake, but I never was fulfilled with just driving out, finding a deer, shooting it and coming back home. I wanted more of a personal challenge.

Another thing that swayed me toward bowhunting was a law change in my home state. Kansas constituted an either/or option for the deer season, giving hunters a choice of hunting with either a gun or a bow. The rifle permits are drawn for, whereas the bow permits are purchased over the counter. Considering my options, it was only natural that I became a bowhunter.

My first attempt at bowhunting was rather futile, to say the least. I tried to bag a deer between the rifle seasons in the fall of 1970, but without any knowledge about cover scents, thermals, deer habits and movements, rubs, scrapes, etc., I had very little luck. I had never had to know about these things before while hunting with a rifle. My interest in bowhunting fizzled a little after that.

That interest in archery was rekindled in 1978 when my sons Wayne and Allen took up bowhunting. The following year, for Father's Day, Wayne bought me a new Jenning's Star Lite compound, and after much practice, I was off on my first serious bowhunt.

Although my first season was unsuccessful, I managed to down a nice eight-point on the third day of my second season. That buck was followed by another eight-point on the first day of my third season. My boys laughingly started referring to me as "One Shot Herron."

Over the years, we have established a few priorities which we feel have contributed to our hunting success. Of course, hunting a good area is always important to consistently fill your tag. But a good relationship with the landowner, we feel, is the most important thing. The rancher who owns the land which we hunt, owns a vast amount of land and we assist him by reporting anything that is out of the ordinary (downed fences, sick cattle, etc.). We also leave things exactly the way we find them. At the end of the season, we always offer him some of the venison.

Our target practice starts in the spring and runs right through deer season. About three weeks before season, we switch to broadheads and practice with them daily. Now that may sound like a lot of practice, and it is, but we make it a family affair. And all of us can hold our own when it comes to making a fatal shot at almost any reasonable range.

In the area that we hunt, we have 15 tree stands placed. This allows us great flexibility when hunting conditions change. They even offer accessibility in foul weather. We recently added two Apache tripods to our stock, extending our mobility even more.

On the evening of November 17, 1984, I placed myself in one of Wayne's new stands, which is built in an area frequently used by big bucks during the rut. Wayne hunted from another stand about 100 yards to the southeast of me, where he had hoped to connect with his fourth Pope & Young'er. I was also going for a trophy, having decided to join Allen and Wayne in their quest for

trophies only. In the two years following that decision, I had passed up a number of opportunities to collect venison, but I was firm in my resolve. I had already spent 77 hours on stand during 1984 and had yet to take a shot.

I had been in my stand for an hour and a half, when I spotted the doe mentioned at the beginning of this story.

The buck was huge. His antlers were so massive that they looked like it would be tiring for him just to hold them up. When he moved his head from side to side, I knew he was a monster.

The rut was on and it was obvious the buck was hot. He pursued the doe, constantly monitoring her for signs of compliance. That was fine with me. The doe was making a beeline for my stand and if the buck followed her I would have an easy shot. Very carefully, I raised my York CNC 50-pound bow and made ready for the draw. Almost as if on cue, the doe appeared silently below me. My heart raced as I awaited the buck, who would, at any minute, appear for a perfect shot.

Movement to my left caught my eye. It was the buck! For some reason or other, he didn't follow the doe through the tamaracks. Instead, he had chosen a path out the other side that offered no shot because of the thick brush between us. I noticed the tiny clearing just moments before I panicked. It was in front of the buck—and it looked like he would pass through it! I drew my bow and waited for his crossing. I released my favorite flying XX75 tipped with a Savora three-bladed broadhead as soon as he cleared the brush.

All of the practice paid off. The arrow slammed into the buck and exited the other side. I was a bit surprised when the buck didn't run, but merely turned and walked calmly out of sight. A few minutes later, Wayne came running up. He had heard my arrow hit and knew that I had shot a deer. We waited a bit, then started trailing him.

The blood trail lead to the south. It was heavy, so I expected to find the buck after every step. When we accidentally kicked the buck up about 200 yards later, I started to worry. Maybe my shot wasn't as good as it looked. It was best to give him some more time. We decided to go to town and eat some dinner before continuing.

Allen and my wife, Maxine, joined our search after dinner. The trail was much longer than I anticipated it would be. First, we trailed him north to the river, which was a good half mile away. At the river, the trail turned east for another half mile before turning south again. We were back almost to our starting point.

Kansas farm country bucks grow big. Proof is Ralph Herron's whitetail that scores 164⅞ Pope & Young points.

By this time, the blood trail was sparse and we often had to resort to searching for sign on our hands and knees. Wayne, Allen and I had tracked many deer over the years, but this one had us in a tizzy. We had just reached the point of total despair, when Maxine called out, "Here he is!" She found him while we were still picking through the leaves on our hands and knees!!! He was hit through the liver.

After the 60-day drying period, my buck scored an official 164⅞ Pope & Young points. My trophy of a lifetime.

36

Cougar On A Coyote Hunt

by Walt Earl, Sr.

A s I topped the ridge I took a deep breath and tried to hear my dogs. Between the pounding of my heart and the slight breeze that was blowing, I thought I could heard them, but wasn't sure. My hunting partner for this trip was Bud Colby, who lived south of Harlowton, Montana. When he caught up with me, he said he could hear the dogs and they were barking treed!

This hunt started with me dropping by Bud's place and asking him to go for a ride with me to try and call a coyote or two. Bud told his wife, Randy, that he would be home by 1:00 p.m. I knew better.

I had just happened to throw my dogs, Annia, Rowdy and Maybelle in the dog box in the back of my pickup. I raise Redbone hounds and have had my own bloodline for several years. They will do what I want and that is all that matters.

Bud and I headed up in to the the Little Belt Mountains, which just happened to have a fair snow cover. It hadn't snowed for three days and it was around 10 degrees above zero—perfect conditions for calling coyotes. Actually, it wasn't bad for lion hunting either.

As we were driving up to Sawmill Canyon, Bud asked me why I had brought the dogs along. I said, ''Just in Case.'' We checked for tracks as we drove through Sawmill, then picked out a likely spot and tried to call coyotes. No luck in either category. We then headed for Antelope Canyon and as our luck would have it, we found a good-sized lion track! It was over 24 hours old, but I turned the dogs loose just in case. They took off, leaving Bud and I way behind them.

After following the tracks awhile, we came upon the place where the big tom had stalked a herd of elk. The whole story was written in the snow. We could see where the cat had first seen the elk feeding, turned downwind and headed towards them from the east. The closer the cat got, the shorter his stride. Every now and then he would flatten himself in the snow, leaving behind little triangles where his twiching tail has brushed across the snow. When he got within 30 yards of the elk, he lay behind a small fir tree for quite some time. He had shifted his weight dozens of times, completely packing the snow where he stood.

From the looks of the elk tracks, there must have been 10 or 12 animals in the herd. As elk hunting is for man, it is for the big cat. If you have 12 elk, you must contend with 24 eyes, 24 ears and 12 very sensitive noses. Add it up, and man or cat have a one in 60 chance of taking one of them.

It, evidently, was not the time or the day for the cat to take one of the elk. The elk left, probably after spotting a slight movement from the cougar or maybe catching his scent. The big tom never had an opportunity to make his deadly attack. His track showed that he walked away from the fleeing elk. Had he been able to go at the elk, it would have been quite a match. Imagine a 160-pound animal moving about 30 miles an hour striking a stationary animal. I've personally seen the evidence of such an attack and am sure it is over quickly for an elk or deer. Most of the time it appears the quarry is dropped in its tracks, unaware of what hit them.

After we walked for an hour or so, we came upon the ridge and could hear the dogs. From there, it took about one-half hour of slipping and sliding down one hill and crawling up another. In all it was three-quarters of a mile up and down, but only 300 yards straight across.

The big cat was in a 40-foot fir tree and seemed content to stay there awhile. I asked Bud to stay with the dogs while I went to the top of the ridge to see how far away the pickup truck was. As I topped the ridge, I thought I heard the dogs raising more cain than when I left them, but being a little hard of hearing, I couldn't tell. I found out how far away the truck was, and headed back to Bud and the dogs.

When I made it back to the tree, the dogs and cat were gone. By listening closely, I could hear the dogs barking treed a short way down a coulee to my right. I started heading in that direction using the dog and cat tracks as a guide, but was puzzled when I noticed Bud's tracks were nowhere to be seen, I hollered a couple of times and heard a faint voice behind me. Bud stepped out from behind some brush and his eyes were as big as coffee cups. I asked him what had happened and he said a gust of wind came up and started shaking the tree. "He must have spotted me and thought I was shaking the tree because he looked at me and started down the tree. I turned and got the hell out of there," Bud said. Bud was kind of shaken over what had happened as he was unarmed. It was the first live cat he had ever seen.

When the cat reached the ground, the dogs formed a semi-circle around him, but the cat broke through the ring and ran to a rock ledge, which he climbed up and over. We wasted no time following the dogs and soon came upon the cat 16 feet up in a large ponderosa pine. I got right under the tree and asked Bud to give me a hand with the dogs and camera. He told me, without mincing words, where I could go and how fast I could go there. Some of the adjectives he called me and the cat are just not true...

After taking several pictures, I put everything into my backpack. Then I looked the cat over and started to realize just how big he really was. I could tell that if he didn't make the book, he would be awful close. I told Bud I was going to take the cat, as I had my lion tag with me.

Bud told me again, from quite a distance, just what I could do with the cat. Boy, were some of his expressions ever embarassing.

I tied the dogs back and shot the cat in the ribs with my Ruger .22 pistol and he was dead before he hit the ground. Only then did my hunting buddy come close enough to take my picture with the cat. We were a mile and a half from the road and six miles from the truck if we took the easy way out. We could cut that distance in half if we cut cross-country. I asked Bud if he would like to stay with the cougar along the side of the road while I went to retrieve the truck. I was told in no uncertain terms that he would not be left behind with a cat, dead or alive! "Besides," he reasoned, "it's not that far back to the truck."

We arrived back at my house just before dark. Bud phoned his wife immediately to let her know he was on his way home. We then weighed and measured the cat. It dressed out at 167 pounds and measured seven foot, nine inches from the tip of his nose to the end of his tail. His skull measured 141$\frac{4}{16}$ a couple months later, just $\frac{2}{16}$ shy of going into Boone and Crockett.

After caring for the dogs, Bud asked if my wife and kids would

When outfitter Walt Earl, Sr. headed out to hunt coyotes on a cold, crisp morning, he never expected to come home at the end of the day with a trophy like this.

like to go over to his place to visit. We got to his place and he was forgiven for being late because his wife is a good ole girl. They invited us to stay over for supper. It was then we heard Bud's side of the story. I thought my sides were going to split when he, of course, left out some of the descriptive adjectives he had used while on the mountain. To this day, he can do a good job of telling his story. I doubt the cat wanted a piece of his tough ole body anyway.

37

Last Minute Alaskan Hunt

by Gary Brown

It was a sight every big game hunter dreams of. I had stalked within 150 yards of a herd of 75-80 caribou. I could hardly believe my eyes. There were 42 mature bulls that I could see—most of them were bedded down with only the top of their racks visible above the lush tundra grass. The closest one was a nice mature bull standing broadside 150 yards away. Though I was into the last hour of a three-week unguided Alaskan hunt, I didn't raise my rifle. Having already taken a nice bull in 1984, I wanted a *real* trophy. The racks of the bedded bulls that were only partially visible drew my attention. After about 10 minutes of glassing, I narrowed my choice to four bulls. I would wait for one of those four to stand.

My hunt on the Alaskan Peninsula came quite unexpectedly. When I had pulled the trigger and dropped my 54-inch moose four days earlier, I thought my hunting for this trip was over. But after I got all the moose meat to the processor in Anchorage, I still had four full days until my plane would leave to take me back to my home in Grand Rapids, Michigan. So I called a pilot friend, somehow hoping that he had plans to go hunting since he had some time off. He informed me that he wouldn't be going, but that three of his friends were leaving in two planes the next day to go caribou hunting on the Alaska Peninsula. A couple of phone calls later, I was invited to go along if I paid my share of the gas. Since they were only planning to hunt a couple of days and I still had an unfilled caribou tag, I jumped at the chance.

We left Saturday afternoon and followed each other on the beautiful flight through the mountains by way of Lake Clark Pass. We landed in Kakhonak, a small Eskimo village on Lake Iliamna, to deliver groceries to a school teacher friend of one of the pilots. The teacher gave us a quick tour of the village and treated us to cooked salmon spread and crackers before we were off again. We landed on an unmarked gravel bar near Lake Becharof. By the time we anchored the airplanes down and set up camp, it was dark and time to hit the bags. I found it very hard to get to sleep that night because a fierce wind howled all night and threatened to shred my little pup tent. I also wondered where the large sow grizzly and her three cubs that we had seen from the air were. After all, we had spotted them only about a half mile from our camp and they were on the move. When I finally got to sleep, I dreamed of large herds of caribou and big racked bulls.

I woke Sunday morning at 6:45 and headed out for the day's hunt with all three of my companions still in bed. I covered many miles of tundra swamp and low hills and glassed thousands of acres during the course of the day, but only spotted a cow and calf caribou, a cow and calf moose and the highlight of the day—a sow grizzly with three cubs. I watched them feed and play for 45 minutes before moving on. My companions hadn't done any better although two of them did get shots at caribou.

The weather turned worse overnight. A steady rain and thick fog greeted us in the morning. When my alarm went off at 7:30, I couldn't see 30 yards. Our plans were to try to leave around 10:00 a.m., but I knew the weather wouldn't permit it. I headed out into the thick fog alone, hoping that maybe it would lift or that I might "run into" a herd of caribou. After all, this was my last chance to fill my caribou tag.

By 10 o'clock, the fog had lifted enough that I thought the pilots might want to take off, so I headed back to camp. I was only several hundred yards from camp when I spotted the herd of caribou about three-quarters of a mile away. It was still too foggy to tell whether there were any good bulls, so I stalked closer. The first quarter mile went easy and then I could make out antlers—lots of them. In spite of the steady drizzle, I dropped my rain gear and day pack for the final stalk. The stalk was mostly crawling as there is very little cover on the open tundra. It took a full hour to cover the last 600-700 yards to the position where I started this story.

To me, the best part of hunting is observing wildlife in its natural habitat. While I waited for one of the four bulls to rise, I sure got a treat. Several fights and shoving matches were going on with some of the lesser bulls. At one time, six bulls were fighting in one bunch. I watched a lone cow walk through the bedded bulls and several got up and chased her. Different bulls would occasionally stand and feed awhile then lay down again. Any of these bulls were trophies by most hunters' standards. Each time a bull stood, my rifle would come up, and then I would decide that it wasn't the biggest one. I laid in the small depression in the steady drizzle observing the herd for 55 minutes before one of my "chosen four" finally stood. As the big bull stretched in all his glory, my familiar 7.65 Argentine Mauser was brought to my shoulder with confidence and I started to squeeze the trigger. I held off. I still wanted a better look at the others. The same scene was repeated a second time when another of the "chosen four" stood.

By this time, most of the herd stood up and were slowly feeding up the hill. Finally, the third bull of the "chosen four" stood up and started moving up the hill. Again, my rifle came to my shoulder, but this time I didn't hesitate. I found the lung area in my scope and squeezed the trigger. The 175-grain Speer round nose pushed by 42 grains of IMR 4895 powder flew perfectly and dropped the bull in his tracks.

After quickly field dressing my bull, I headed for camp. It was 1:15 and I was worried that my friends were waiting for me before taking off. As it turned out, they had also killed two bulls. When I shot my bull, the herd ran toward my partners two of them were able to bring down bulls. We all met back at camp and grabbed our backpacks and cameras and headed back out; my three companions went to their two bulls and I took off after mine. I got 174 pounds of boned meat off of my bull, and I was able to carry that plus the head, cape and antlers back to camp in two trips. I got another wildlife treat when a red fox came right up to within 10 yards of me and started eating scraps from the carcass while I was loading my pack.

We had all three caribou back in camp by 6:30. With an overcast sky and only two hours of daylight remaining, we decided to wait until the next morning and hope for better weather to take off. The pilots were expecting a hard time getting off the small gravel bar so we spent the rest of the day draining extra fuel from the tanks and clearing boulders from the end of the strip.

The weather the next morning wasn't any better, so we just killed time around camp waiting for the weather to clear. By 1:00 the sky had cleared enough to take off, so we flew to King Salmon and inquired at the flight tower there about the weather between us and Anchorage. Against their advice, we decided to try to "poke" our way through. We were able to fly under the clouds and we encountered only mild turbulence. My pilot friends were experienced and we landed at Merrill Field in Anchorage just at sunset.

I was up until 3:00 a.m. that night packing my 16 pieces of "luggage" for the flight home. After only two hours of sleep, I was up again and off to the Anchorage Airport for my flight back home.

Those last four days of my three-week unguided hunt in Alaska could be summed up as beautiful, exciting, scary, dangerous, tiresome, delightful, hectic, entertaining, but most of all, a perfect end to a wonderful hunt.

38

Hot Weather Blacktail

by Kenzia Drake

I have taken whitetail and mule deer bucks before, but I still consider the blacktail to be the most elusive of the three. Part of the reason is that here in California, we hunt a season that is late in the summer; long before the rut. During this early season the ground is dry and noisy and daytime temperatures often exceed 100 degrees. The deer just don't move around.

The dense brush the deer inhabit also gives them an advantage; one step and they're out of there. Good bucks just don't leave the brush and get caught in the open.

Raising a family (I often have my seven and nine year old daughters along on my hunts) requires a steady work schedule, so I normally hunt on weekends. The Columbus Day three-day weekend is one of the few that falls during the season and I usually hunt it, but this particular season one of my friends decided to get married on that Saturday. That weekend was also the opening of bear season. Despite the very late start on Saturday (I even sneaked away from the reception early) my hunting partner, Frank Rembert, and his two sons and I arrived at our camp in time to hunt an hour before darkness fell.

We were hunting in Mendocino County, a few miles south of Covelo. The terrain is steep, brush and oak covered. It drains into the Eel River.

After dark, we set up our tent, had a bite to eat and went to bed so we could get up early the next morning.

Sunday morning Frank shot a nice black bear. Sunday evening I managed to connect on one with a beautiful blond coat. One 150-grain Nosler Solid Base handload from my Browning .30-06 did the trick.

Monday morning, Frank wanted to hunt down a long canyon that appeared tough enough to discourage most other hunters from trying it. It was my turn to take the Jeep around to the bottom. We agreed to meet at the river at 11:00.

When Frank was getting his gear ready to leave, I spotted three deer about 2,000 yards above us along the edge of a fairly open bowl. Even with binoculars I could see no horns, but one of the deer was much larger and darker than the other two. I told Frank that I was going to hike up towards the deer to get a better look at the larger one and that I'd see him at the bottom.

I hunted up a side ridge out of sight of the bowl where the deer were. When I got up to where I figured the deer to be, I carefully looked over the ridge and there, about 200 yards away from me was a huge buck staring straight at me! Only my head was above the ridge, but somehow he spotted me. I ducked out of sight and crawled over the ridge with my rifle ready. When I got my barrel above the weeds (he was still watching me) I took my time and aimed. I wanted to make my first shot count.

At the shot, the buck spun around and ran out of sight. I felt my shot was on the mark so I wasn't worried about losing him. I picked up my empty brass and walked over to where I had last seen him.

There was blood everywhere—but no deer. When I looked up I spotted a huge buck and a doe. They immediately exploded toward the nearest trees. I wondered if he was my buck, but it seemed his rack was wider but not as tall as the buck I had shot at. I hoped that he wasn't the buck I had already shot.

I started following the blood trail and in a few yards saw dark, heavy antlers sticking above the weeds. There lay the finest buck I've ever seen. My shot, a little farther forward than I tried to place it, had severed one of the arteries in the base of his neck.

As I cleaned him out I admired the phenomenal beauty of the animal and thought how often I had found large shed antlers and always said "I hope I can take one like this some day!" I guess "some day" was here.

I drove down to the river to meet Frank. When he said he heard me shoot, I blurted out: "He might make the book."

Temperatures often push 100 degrees during the California blacktail season, but that didn't deter Ken Drake from taking this trophy with a neck shot at 200 yards. The rack scores 138²/₈

That night at home, a rough "green score" showed the buck should exceed the magical 130 point mark. After the mandatory 60-day drying period, he was officially scored at 138⅜ points. He is certainly not a new record, but this buck is the best I've taken so far.

Chances are slim that I'll ever take a better blacktail, but even if I don't, this one is just fine for my once-in-a-lifetime buck!

39

10 Years And $50,000 Later

by Joe Riveira

Ten years before I got my record book bull I made up my mind that the first elk I would shoot would be the one I would hang on the wall. My friend and hunting partner Burt Marles is also a trophy elk hunter and felt the same way. We have elk hunted together for the past six years. Burt lives in Illinois and I in Florida, so we planned to meet in Calgary, Alberta, on November 8, 1986. Our outfitters, J.W. Campshell and Edith Magy picked us up that night and we spent the night at their house in Dedsburg.

The next morning we loaded up eight horses and enough supplies to last a couple of weeks and headed for the high country. Three hours later we unloaded the horses, gear and packs and headed for the main camp at Forbidden Creek, high in the Canadian Rockies. Five hours later, and way after dark, we arrived in camp, where we spent the next few hours unpacking, feeding the horses and scaring a hungry grizzly out of camp, but not necessarily in that order.

To prepare myself for this hunt, I ran anywhere from five to seven miles a day, a few months before I had left. So between my running and trapping alligators, I would be in fair shape (for an old man) come hunting season.

The next few days were spent scouting. All four of us would take off in the morning and then split up and compare our findings every evening. We would see anywhere from 50 to 100 elk every day, several of them legal 5x5s, but nothing we wanted to take.

We decided a few days later we would pack a few items and set up a spike camp in the Cutoff Creek area about three hours from our main camp. We had seen several lone bulls in the area, so we figured it was the best place to find a real monster.

The 14th of November dawned very cold with plenty of snow. We got up at 4 a.m. and ate a hearty meal (you need a lot of fuel in this country). We saddled up and hunted hard all day. We saw a few lone bulls, but still nothing we wanted.

The next day, we left camp a little ahead of schedule and rode together for a couple of hours. J.W. and Burt would check one mountain and Edi and I would check the other. It was cold, the thermometer read almost 40 below zero and the wind had to be blowing 25 to 30 knots by the time the sun came up.

I was riding a few feet behind Edi when I heard her whisper, "Joe there's a bull at the edge of the timber line rubbing his antlers on a tree," while pointing to the edge of the timber. The bull was enormous. I knew immediately he was the one I wanted. With the wind blowing in my favor, I removed first my scope caps, then my shooting hand glove. I dismounted, and took off in a low crouch in the direction of the bull. All of a sudden I fell in a hole, plunging past my waist in snow. I raised my gun to check the scope and found it full of snow. When I finally cleared it, the bull was walking casually into the timber. I was out of breath from struggling in the snow and my heart was going a mile a minute. I had to hurry!

I brought the crosshairs down on him and shot, catching the bull low in the right shoulder. I worked the bolt and pulled the trigger a second time. I couldn't believe it when the gun went click. When I raised the gun to grab the bolt and eject the shell, it fired into the ground in front of me. My adrenalin was really flowing by the time I pulled the trigger a third time. It missed.

Just then the bull stopped broadside and turned to look at us. Edi whispered desperately "Shoot Joe, shoot!" I couldn't, I was out of shells! I shoot a 7mm Remington Magnum which holds three shells in the magazine and one in the chamber. I always leave the chamber empty when hunting on horseback.

I tried to remove a shell from my cartridge belt holder, but I couldn't because the cold had robbed me of control of my right hand. My fingers wouldn't function. I tried to reach my cartridge belt with my left hand but couldn't reach it. The elk finally walked off.

The first thing that came to mind was I had blown the chance of a lifetime I had been waiting the last 10 years for. The fact that I had wounded the bull made me feel even worse. I looked at Edi and she looked like I felt, like hell.

We mounted the horses and lit out as fast as we could. The wind was blowing so hard that the tracks were being blown away. Every now and then the elk would stop and leave a blood trail. We followed as far as we could by horse. We had come to a steep shale mountainside that had to be followed on foot. We followed the bull about two miles when we decided we would not push him any farther and hoped he would bed down. It was a good decision.

I went back to the horses and rode around the mountain in an attempt to get in front of the elk. Edi would wait a couple of hours then continue to track the bull and hopefully push him by me. I positioned myself where we figured the elk would pass. I could see a few clearings about 300 to 400 yards below me. It was now about 4:30 p.m. The wind had slowed down to about 15 to 20 knots, but it was still very cold.

Moments of the hunt were still going around in my mind when all of a sudden I noticed a movement about 450 yards out. The first clearing he would have to clear was about 400 yards. This time I removed my glove and waited. The first shot caught him in the rear part of the rib cage. My second shot, taken when he hit the second clearing about 350 yards out, caught him in the front of the rib cage and took out both lungs. He was out of sight before I could fire a third time, but I knew I had hit him hard even though he never slowed down.

It took me 20 to 30 minutes to reach the area the large bull lay. I will never forget that moment. I didn't realize until I got up close as to the size of this magnificent animal. He later scored 393⅛.

It was way after dark when we finished caping out my bull. We got the cape and antlers as high as we possibly could in a tree to keep the grizzlies or wolves from hauling them off. While caping, we built a fire to keep from freezing. We also broke through the ice on a creek to get some water. The water felt almost warm.

The next biggest chore was yet to come — getting back to camp. We decided to come back the next day and pack him out, but that was tomorrow. Today we had to go about three miles to where we had left the horses, and those three miles were straight up. I was never more glad to see a horse in my life. I swore I would never say that, but he was a sight for sore eyes.

It was well past midnight when we finally made it back to

Joe Riveira, left, poses with a hard-won trophy. It took 10 years, but he finally got the one he wanted in his sights.

camp that night. I was so exhausted by that time I wanted to skip dinner and head straight for the sack. We had a light dinner before turning in. We slept until 7:00 a.m. the next morning, had a hearty breakfast and were ready to start all over again.

I stayed in camp that day to set a few martin traps, which really was a waste of time because the birds were tripping all of them. It was nothing like trapping alligators. Meanwhile Burt, J.W., Edi and Bill would go out and pack out my bull. It took them almost nine hours. That evening we had a feast and a half. We ate elk liver and backstrap. This was the second most memorable part of the hunt.

Edi and I returned to the main camp that evening to get some more supplies. When we returned the following day, Burt and J.W. said they had made it back to camp at 4 a.m. They had spent the night caping out another 6x6 bull that later scored 356. And it wasn't the largest one they had seen! It sure was a beautiful animal.

40

Backpack Hunt
For Moose And Griz

by Toby Johnson

We could see four bulls in a valley that sprawled below our vantage point on top of the mountain. The first bull was bedded down in a patch of alders quietly surveying his surroundings. Another one was slowly feeding his way across the valley floor, while a third bull stood still as a statue.

I wanted the fourth bull. It was by far the biggest of the four, with good width and massive palms, but it was also the farthest away.

It was the last day of a 10-day combination moose and grizzly backpack hunt with Rick Furniss and Emil McCook of Kechika Range Outfitters, Ltd. in northern British Columbia. I arrived in base camp on Weisner Lake on August 31 from Watson Lake, Yukon, by chartered plane. My guide and I flew into another lake about five miles from camp the next day. From there, we were on our own for the next 10 days. Everything we needed was on our backs.

The area was prime grizzly bear country. A massive forest fire had ripped through the area some 40 years earlier, leaving behind burnt brush and cleared land—perfect conditions for blueberries.

Blueberries and bears go together like peaches and cream, so I knew it was only a matter of time before a bruin wandered into the huge berry patch. Glassing for them was enjoyable, as dinner was only a handful away.

I took a grizzly on the evening of the third day, in the way I always dreamed of getting one. I was glassing the hillsides, when I located him on a distant ridge. I made the stalk and killed him with a 300 yard shot. He was a beautiful boar, with silver tips over a dark, black hide that squared seven feet, two inches. The Fish and Game Department informed me later that he was five years old.

My guide and I decided to hike back to base camp with my bear, instead of carrying the hide and head with us for the duration of the hunt. It took us two days to get back to Weisner Lake, about a six-mile hike. We were carrying quite a load, so we took our time and hunted as we went. Along the way, we encountered four or five spruce grouse, which flew out of the brush directly in front of us. Since I was always thinking grizzly, the grouse scared the hell out of me.

On September 7, we hiked out of base camp to make a one-day hunt instead of heading back to a spike camp. We spotted a nice moose that day, but couldn't get close enough for a shot. It felt good to come back that evening to a home cooked meal and a soft bed. I was getting tired of eating freeze-dried food and I was stiff from sleeping on the hard ground.

The next day we headed out of camp with our packs on. We had two days left to hunt and we were going to give it everything we had.

The ninth day was a bust. We spent a lot of time glassing valley floors and brushy patches, but never spotted a moose.

The last day dawned cold, wet and miserable. A storm had blown in from the north, rattling our tent enough to keep us awake most of the night. We were up early, broke camp and headed out for our last attempt to get a big Canadian moose.

Our first stop was a point that overlooked a number of valleys and hillsides. It was there we spotted the four bulls we were now watching.

The big bull was obviously entering the rut because he thrashed his antlers on every bush and tree he came to. He was heading our way, so my guide and I simply sat there and watched him through our spotting scopes. We lost sight of him from time to time as he moved in and out of the brush. At times, 20 minutes would pass before we saw him again. Finally, he disappeared from sight. We spent the next hour wondering where he had gone.

Suddenly, he appeared near one of the other bulls!

My guide and I talked the situation over. The moose was still about a mile away, but now the other bulls were behind him. We

decided that I should attempt a stalk while my guide stayed and watched from above.

As I made my way down the wind-swept mountainside, I couldn't help but notice how thick all the willows, brush and alders were. It sure didn't appear that way, looking down from the mountain top. I started wondering if I would be able to see the moose when I got close enough.

When I finally reached the area the moose had been, I conducted a thorough ground-level search for the bull. When that failed, I resorted to climbing trees in the area. Even that didn't help. I finally looked back up the mountain, hoping to get a clue about the bull's whereabouts from my guide. I could see that he had built a fire, so I figured the moose had left the area and my guide had built a fire to keep warm.

I decided to call it quits and head back up the mountain. I didn't make it. The smaller of the two bulls suddenly ran out the back side of a small ridge I was on. I hesitated a few moments, praying that the other moose would follow him. Sure enough, about a minute later, the bull came out and stopped about 100 yards away. My first shot caught him through the lungs. My second got him in the neck.

When I walked up to the bull, I could see he was a real trophy; the bull I had dreamed about when I had booked the hunt. I was pretty sure he would make Boone and Crockett, but wouldn't know until I scored him. So I grabbed my tape measure and started calculating. My numbers weren't precise, but I knew when I finished that he would score over 200. The minimum score needed for the record book is 195 points. I had the bull rescored when the drying period ended 60 days later. The bull officially scored 201⅜, good enough to place 153rd in the all-time list at the time.

41

Then Came Success

by Norman Truelove

The two does startled me when they bounded from their beds only 100 yards from me. My heart jumped, but my permit said "Buck only!" I lowered my gun and watched them wave good-bye with their big white tails.

Deer season is an exciting time for our family. My dad takes his vacation from work and my uncle cuts his farming chores to a minimum. I, unfortunately, hunt only the weekends because I'm still in school.

All of our deer hunting is done on the farm land surrounding our home in Hartford, Kansas. During the first two days of the season, I spent hours sitting in a hedge tree on my uncle's farm. A creek with plenty of timber for cover passes through the farm and deer often go through the area in the mornings and evenings.

Opening day, a six-pointer passed within 100 yards of me. Cold weather, a twitchy trigger finger and plenty of excitement all resulted in a complete miss! The deer turned and started running straight for the tree I was sitting in. He turned broadside about 50 feet away. I shot again, but missed a second time.

I was very upset with myself by that time. I did manage to stay in the tree and watch the deer moving to the east. I noticed my uncle coming across the field. He spotted the buck and snapped off a shot as it disappeared. He also missed. Both of us headed back to the house for food and warmth, and to share our misery.

The second day of the season was a complete bust. We hunted the same area but, contrary to our hopes, the buck didn't show himself again. I was disheartened. I had to go back to school in the morning and wouldn't be able to hunt until late in the afternoon. Still, it was good to get out of the bitter wind that plagued us all day.

As predicted, my classroom work received very little attention the next day. During first hour, I kept thinking about the six-pointer I missed. I spent the next two planning my afternoon hunt. Hours three and four were spent reliving a great shot I made on a monster buck that lives in the back of my mind. I stared at the clock for the last hour. I wanted to get a buck!

When the dismissal bell rang, I hurdled my desk and headed out the door at top speed. At home, I quickly changed into my hunting clothes and grabbed my rifle. My uncle was waiting for me.

We decided to try another area to the south. My uncle had seen several deer there while harvesting several weeks earlier. I was so wired by the time we made it into the timber, my heart nearly stopped when we jumped two does on the way to our stands. Our permits were good for bucks only, so we had to let them go. We knew the does had blown our cover for the day and were sure that our chances of seeing a buck were slim, but we continued on anyway.

There was only one hour of legal hunting time remaining by the time we selected our stands. I chose an old walnut on the west side of a draw. My uncle found a hedge tree southeast of me and on the opposite side of the draw. Half an hour went by. Nothing showed but a bunch of woodpeckers, bluejays and squirrels. Suddenly an enormous buck appeared—and he was heading straight toward the tree I was in! I immediately raised my rifle to my shoulder. The buck must have spotted me because he froze and stared in my direction. I took advantage of the situation and hurriedly squeezed the trigger. The buck wheeled and bounded away in a frantic retreat.

"Did you hit him?" my uncle hollered.

"I should have," I yelled back as I scrambled down the tree.

We met where the buck was standing when I shot. There was no blood or hair in the immediate area, but I felt good about my shot. We started following the buck's tracks. We found the first pool of blood 50 feet later. It sent my heart into my throat. We continued on. Rounding the next thicket I spotted him. The biggest

buck I had ever seen was laying in the grass in front of me. My dream had come true!

All the frustration of opening day was forgotten in seconds. My uncle slapped me on the back, congratulating me on a fine shot. The story telling began.

Uncle Earl had seen the buck first and, unknown to me, had been following the buck in his sights. The buck stopped when he apparently heard my uncle move into a better shooting position. Lucky for me, the buck was in my sights by that time. He was hidden from my uncle's view by a tree.

"Three more steps and he would have been mine," Earl informed me. Excitement runs very high at a time like this!

My uncle stayed with the buck while I drove the two miles to get my Dad. Dad knew when I came flying down the road, horn blaring, that I had shot a deer. After a month and a half of bowhunting himself, Dad was ready to get in on the action.

The three of us then dragged the carcass to the waiting pickup. Upon arrival at the locker plant, we found the carcass was too big for them to weigh without completely dressing it. The dressed carcass weighed 152 pounds. We also found a bowhunter's broadhead in the buck's front shoulder blade, but it apparently didn't bother him much. Some other hunter must have faced the same disappointment I had on opening day. Unlike him, I had a second chance and wound up with a winning buck.

42

My Friend Had The First Shot

by George Poleshock

In June of 1979 I booked a 1980 Quebec-Labrador caribou hunt with Wedge Hills Lodge, located along the north section of the George River, 50 miles south of Ungava Bay, Quebec, Canada.

The next 15 months went very slowly. I spent most of the time reading and studying whatever I could about the caribou. The most important thing to learn was how to judge and know a good caribou in the field.

On Friday morning, September 19, I left my home in Landisburg, Pennsylvania, and headed to Concord, New Hampshire to meet a fellow hunter. Saturday morning we then loaded all our gear into my friend's pickup truck. We traveled 785 miles to Sept-Isles, Quebec, Canada, stayed overnight and the next morning traveled Quebec-Air flying into Schefferville, Quebec. Monday morning, the outfitter met us in his plane, for the last 170 miles.

Tuesday morning I met my guide for the hunt. At the lodge they operate two hunters per guide. My friend from Concord and I teamed up together with the same guide. The guide was a French-Canadian and spoke fair English.

After breakfast we loaded our hunting gear into a raft powered by an outboard motor. The guide said we would travel upriver about four and a half to five miles. There was a cold rain falling and the wind was really blowing, making high waves and rough water. I soon found out why we were told to put on the life jackets before starting up the river in the raft. The section of river we had to travel contained two bad sections of rapids.

When we reached the area we were to hunt in, we went ashore and began glassing the mountains around us. I saw about 25 caribou that morning, but they were either too far away to judge their size or were closer but carried no trophy antlers.

As late afternoon was coming on, we finally saw a small herd of caribou on the mountain about a half mile from us. They were working down the mountain and coming directly for us. From a distance there seemed to be two or three good bulls in the herd.

The guide knew what open area the caribou would probably go through, so we began sneaking back into the higher timber, and then ran some 300 yards back through the trees so we would cut the caribou off. When we got to the large open area, sure enough, the herd of caribou were starting to come through. But all that came through were eight young caribou.

The large bulls, that we had seen earlier with the herd, were nowhere in sight. My friend from New Hampshire decided to take one of the young bulls. As he shot, I watched his caribou stumble and fall. Just then the guide quickly got my attention and pointed to the trees where the younger caribou had come from. My heart started pumping in high gear. About 225 yards away, three good bulls broke out of the timber at a run. As I put my rifle scope on them I could see all three were exceptionally large bulls, but one bull stood out from the rest. This bull carried a large set of antlers that had double shovels in front, high tines on top and carried back points. When my .30-06 Sako cracked, the bull stopped running, stood a second and fell over. He was dead.

We worked the rest of that day getting the caribou back to the river and loaded into the raft. The trip downriver to camp didn't seem quite as bad and rough as it was in the morning. Maybe it was because we were traveling with the current or maybe it was because all I could think of was the fine caribou that I had taken.

When I got back to Pennsylvania, I waited for the 60-day drying period on my caribou antlers, and then took them to be scored by an official Boone and Crockett scorer. I was sure hoping that the antlers would score over 375, the minimum for entry into the record book. To my delight they scored 415⅝, putting my trophy quite high in the Quebec-Labrador caribou category.

43

President's Trophy Winner

"I'm Glad They Got My Scent"

by Bill Hobbs

It was only the second week of September, but it was already cold and windy with snow flurries. Weather only Alaska could have that early in the year. I was hunting with fellow NAHC member Kirby Records from Portland, Oregon, who I met through the Swap Hunt listing in *Keeping Track*, and Don DePaul from Philadelphia, Pennsylvania. We were on a three-week bow and arrow hunt for moose, caribou and black bear in the beautiful Brooks Range of Alaska.

I had yet to draw an arrow as I had been letting Kirby and Don do all the stalking and shooting at what few caribou we had seen. The weather and the caribou were both working against us during the hunt. The day I got my caribou turned out to be one of the nicest days of the hunt, in more ways than one.

We crossed the river by canoe at daybreak, planning to hunt the rolling hills behind camp. Those plans changed when I spotted two bull caribou feeding in the willows along the river as I stepped out of the canoe. I immediately motioned to Don and Kirby that two bull caribou were nearby, and to begin their stalk. Don simply handed me my bow and said "Go for it!" I didn't argue.

The stalk started out beautifully with me down-wind and the caribou feeding and moving towards me. I crept as close as possible, but ran out of cover. The caribou fed by me about 80 yards away, heading downstream. In the meantime, Kirby and Don decided to leave me with these caribou and hunt their own.

On the next two stalks, I got close enough to the bulls to hear them eating, but something went wrong both times. The first time, I ran out of cover again and had to abandon the stalk. The second time, the bulls turned and walked away from me faster than I could stalk effectively.

My chance finally came when the bulls started feeding again behind a large willow clump near a 90 degree bend in the river. I took off at a run, sprinting about 150 yards in front of them and found a nice spot to wait for them while they fed in my direction. The wind was still in my favor and quick glimpses of antlers told me that my plan was working.

Without warning, the wind changed direction, and started blowing my scent right to the caribou. Both bulls came out of those willows like they were touched with a hot poker! They started to cross the bottom land about 100 yards below me but ran into my trail. It stopped them. They turned and came in my direction with their heads held high and their noses working overtime trying to figure out where I was. They suddenly turned again and started moving to my left, wanting to head into the open tundra. They ran into my trail again, forcing them to head toward me.

Now I had both caribou walking right at me—and only 40 yards away! I knelt in front of a small willow growing in a little depression along a dry creek bed, facing the caribou with an arrow ready. I had made up my mind to shoot the big bull when he got close enough, but wasn't sure he was going to when the smaller bull walked on a little knoll 10 yards away, stopped and looked right at me.

I started to draw on the big bull when he was about 20 yards out. The small bull immediately snorted and turned to run. I couldn't worry about him any longer and quickly aimed at the big bull, releasing when everything looked "right." The arrow caught the big bull behind the last rib as he was making his second bound. I stood up and watched him run about 150 to 175 yards onto the open tundra before going down. To this day I don't know what happened to the other caribou. I never did see where he went after I shot the bigger bull.

I spent close to two to three hours stalking and playing cat and mouse with those two bulls before I took my shot. I'm glad the wind changed and blew my scent to the bulls. How many times have you heard that one?

My bull was the only caribou taken on our hunt. He later

Bill Hobbs' bow-killed caribou scored 366⅜ and was the only bull taken on this Alaskan bow hunt.

scored 366⅜. Kirby arrowed a real nice 55-inch bull moose and Don arrowed a nice black bear. I also arrowed a lynx later in the hunt. We all enjoyed our Alaskan adventure.